Show Up
for
Your Life

Show Up for Your Life

What the girl you'll be
tomorrow wants you to know today

CHRYSTAL EVANS HURST

ZONDERVAN®

ZONDERVAN

Show Up for Your Life
Copyright © 2018 by Chrystal Evans Hurst

Requests for information should be addressed to:
Zondervan, *3900 Sparks Dr. SE, Grand Rapids, Michigan 49546*

Ebook ISBN 978-0-310-7669-3

Library of Congress Cataloging-in-Publication Data
ISBN 978-0-310766834

Scripture quotations, unless otherwise noted, are taken from the Holy Bible, New International Version®, NIV®. Copyright © 1973, 1978, 1984, 2011 by Biblica, Inc.® Used by permission of Zondervan. All rights reserved worldwide. www .Zondervan.com. The "NIV" and "New International Version" are trademarks registered in the United States Patent and Trademark Office by Biblica, Inc.®

Any internet addresses (websites, blogs, etc.) and telephone numbers in this book are offered as a resource. They are not intended in any way to be or imply an endorsement by Zondervan, nor does Zondervan vouch for the content of these sites and numbers for the life of this book.

Published in association with the literary agency of WordServe Literary Group, Ltd. www.wordserveliterary.com.

Interior design: Denise Froehlich

Printed in the United States of America

18 19 20 21 22 /LSC/ 10 9 8 7 6 5 4 3 2 1

Dedication

For Alena

*When I wonder what it looks like for a
young woman to show up for her life...
I think of you.
Keep showing up.
Keep doing you.
Keep resting and believing in the
beauty of whose you are.
and...*

For Wynter

This book is for girls just like you.

Contents

Own Your Life

Embrace Your Life

Develop Your Life

Encourage Your Life

Choose Your Life

Foreword

I grew up different. You know those kids who rock a Winnie the Pooh onesie that doesn't really fit? They love it so much they just have to wear it? That was me. I was a home-schooled preacher's kid with Tourette Syndrome and I was straight up different.

I spent most of my middle and high school years desperately awaiting that inevitable moment when everything about me would begin to blend in with everyone and everything. But eventually, I gave it up. I was tired of being different, but it was so much harder trying to fit in.

Thing is, there was no snap-of-a-finger magical unicorn that showed up to make things easier. So I chose to embrace my quirks, my unique experiences, and the intricacies of my story that I knew full well kept me from getting invited to every party or included in every group text. And I learned to love the girl that God created—quirks and all. I decided to show up for my life!

When I was a desperate and broken-hearted teenager with nothing but a guitar, a melody, and a few anxious prayers, I created a song and was nominated for my first GRAMMY Award. Fun fact: I was really confused . . . a GRAMMY? I call my mom's mother my "Granny." So my mom thought there was going to be an award show for grandmothers. (I didn't really grow up with a lot of television in our house . . .)

Anyway, I went to that award show beaming with joy. I

wore cowboy boots that had a custom-bedazzled job and a hand-sewn Asian-inspired vest over a vintage dress. Designed by my mom, sewn by a dear friend who is also a seamstress. I got a few "what are you wearing?" stares and even a couple of blogs bashing my look, but I'll never forget what it felt like to walk around before and after the show, hearing so many artists and producers make comments about my outfit.

"I've never seen boots at the Grammys. I love it!"

"My wife wants to get a pair of shoes like yours. Where can I get some?"

"What's your name? I've never seen anyone dressed like you before."

For one of the first times in my life I was celebrated for being different—for being ME. I continue to write songs about it, make videos about it, and sometimes I add a lil something to a book about it: *I'm different.* But the beauty is that I was *made* to be different and I own those differences. So were you—made to be different. And when we choose to walk in what sets us apart, we show up for an incredible life that we were destined to live.

Chrystal's words throughout this book are a continual reminder that we have to own our story—show up for our life! We have to trust that God—the Creator of our heart's beat—will give us the strength through the good, the bad, and the ugly. With Him, we can not only love where we are but be on our way to where we want to go. I showed up and I still strive to! It doesn't mean that my life is perfect—or even easy—but it does mean that I live everyday confident in knowing that my story is worth telling and worth living.

Above all, I hope you'll show up too!

Love, Jamie Grace

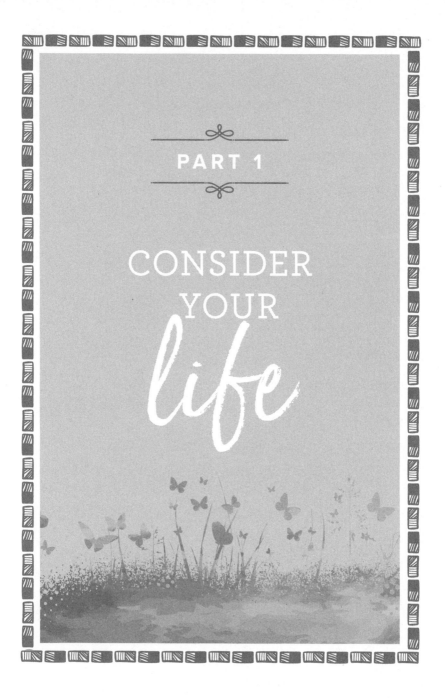

PART 1

CONSIDER YOUR *life*

CHAPTER 1

You Do You

Own your own story

I'd attended a Christian school through eighth grade, so ninth grade was the first year I attended public school. And all I wanted to do was fit in. In each class I'd notice the girls who hurried in to get a front row seat and the ones who beelined for the last row. I'd observe which ones might be new like me and which ones exchanged glances and notes like they'd known each other forever. I was searching for my tribe.

Within about a week I'd started eating lunch with a group of girls who had grown up together. They all bought pizza and fries from the school cafeteria, and I brought apples, yogurt, and my mom's homemade chocolate chip cookies. They all had boyfriends, and I was completely inexperienced in that department. Their language was pretty salty, and the worst words to ever pass my lips were "shut up." Despite our differences, I wanted desperately to fit in.

One day I pulled out a chair at the end of the table, sat

down, and unzipped my red lunch box. The other girls were going off about some teacher they didn't like. Jumping in like I was as streetwise as they were, I wanted them to know I thought that teacher was as horrible as they did.

"I know, right?" I agreed. "She's a #%&*-ing #@*$ *!&#!"

The table fell silent as six pairs of eyes stared at me, shocked at the foul words that had just fallen out of my mouth. Honestly, I was as shocked as anyone.

Finally, one girl broke the silence.

"Girl, don't even. You're not doing it right. Just . . . don't."

I felt my face flush with warmth. I had been trying to be someone I wasn't, and I'd been called out.

So, yeah, it was pretty embarrassing.

That hard lesson has had a lasting impact. Though she acted a little more disgusted than I thought she needed to, that girl was essentially saying: *You do you.* And believe me, I did. I was willing to work on and improve lots of things, but cursing wasn't going to be one of them!

It was better to be *me*, than try to be someone else. And it is better to be *you* than to try to be someone else.

Not long after that, I started looking for a different group of friends to hang out with.

Part of the problem was that I felt self-conscious about being one of the "smart kids." Nothing about "Principal's Gold Star Honor Roll" says, "Here's a cool kid you might want to hang with." Because so many other students weren't interested in achieving academically, I didn't want to be labeled as the smart nerd.

Did I still want to achieve? Yeah, I did. But did I want to stand out among my peers? Nope. Not for being the geeky girl.

But by playing down my gifts and abilities, by failing to honor what made me unique, by trying to blend in with the crowd, I was denying who God had made me to be. I was choosing to sit in the backseat when I should have been gripping the steering wheel of my own life.

You know what it's like to sit in the backseat of the driver's ed car while another kid drives for the first time? When you're not sure if you will live or die? The choices I was making to downplay who I really was should have scared me *that much*.

Being in control of your life really is like driving a car. Whether you're thinking about signing up for driver's ed right now, practicing driving around huge vacant parking lots with your mom, or if you're already pretty confident behind the wheel, I want you to hear that God meant you to be the operator in the driver's seat of your own life. Yes, ultimately, he's in charge, but he's given you this life—and it's yours to choose how it goes.

Until now your parents have been doing a lot of the steering. They decided where you would live, what you would eat, what you would wear, where you'd attend school, and whether you'd attend church. But right now is the season when you are starting to slide into the driver's seat of your own life. Increasingly, you're going to be making more of those choices for yourself. And what I want you to hear is that you are the person who is ultimately responsible for who you will become.

If that sounds like a heavy load, I get it. I've walked in your shoes. And that's exactly why I want to be in this with you. Think of me as that aunt who's teaching you to drive on weekends. I want you to hear that this is your thing, that you're the one behind the wheel, and I want to share with you some of the helpful tips and tools I've picked up along the way—and possibly point out the ditches, hairpin turns, drop-offs, and cliffs you'll want to avoid.

If learning to drive is still ahead of you, and the thought of it freaks you out, let me say it another way: *You are the author of your story and, with God's help, you are responsible for becoming all you can be.* And part of owning that story is not only writing what comes next, but it's accepting and integrating what God has given to you and what's already unfolded. If your parents weren't married when you were born, that's part of your story. If you were reading words off cereal boxes when you were three years old, that's part of your story. If you were diagnosed with childhood cancer when you were five, that's part of your story. If you started singing solos in the church choir at seven, that's part of your story. Some of the pieces of your story are ones you would choose again in a heartbeat. Other parts of your story might be ones you wish had been different. In both cases, God has made the plans and he's poised you to begin writing a beautiful story for the rest of your life once you *own* the chapters that have already been written.

When you take the time to pause and consider your story, you have the greatest ability to notice the pieces you're working with, what you've learned from, what healing work needs to be done, and what choices you want to make to move forward. Denial or half-truths prohibit you from moving forward.

Owning your story is an act of strength.

And if you're not where you want to be today, it doesn't matter so much how you got there as much as it matters that

you acknowledge that where you are is not where you want to be. You are the author . . . so own it.

Part of owning *my* story is owning that I'm a girl who has been raised in the church. I'm a preacher's kid. I know the Bible, and I've had a personal relationship with God for most of my life. I have memorized a few Scriptures in my life, but to be honest, I'm super grateful for Google. Many times I know that certain words are *in* the Bible, but I don't know *exactly* where to find them. But as a young girl my mother made sure I knew this verse in particular: "'For I know the plans I have for you,' declares the

Owning your story is an act of *strength*.

Lᴏʀᴅ, 'plans to prosper you and not to harm you, plans to give you hope and a future'" (Jer. 29:11). I grew up memorizing passages of Scripture that taught me my life could be abundantly full and overflowing (John 10:10 AMP).

I'll give you more of the details later, but there was a moment when I woke up to the realization that my life had veered from the plotline of my expectations. The vision God had given me for my life didn't match my actual life at all. And that's when I had to choose to own my story and re-craft it into one in which I was being all that God had made me to be.

The fact that that was such a difficult season for me is one of the reasons I'm excited to be taking this journey with you. My prayer is that, by exposing some of the ways I lost who I really was, I can spare you some of the struggles I've stumbled through along the way.

As we take this trek together, I want to encourage you to be as honest as you can be. Moving forward begins with telling the truth, the truth that God already knows but wants us to be honest about for the benefit of our own healing. "For He knows the secrets of the heart" (Ps. 44:21).

It takes courage to admit that

- You've experienced hurts you wouldn't have chosen.
- You want something different for your life than what you've seen around you.
- You really don't know what's in your future.
- You may not know how to achieve the dreams in your heart.

I know what I'm talking about when I say that it takes Someone outside of ourselves to reset what's broken, put back together what's been fractured, give us a vision for a beautiful future, and give us the courage, determination, and tools to go after it.

ॐ

What about your story?

Maybe you haven't seen examples of a strong healthy marriage, but that's something you want for your life.

Maybe you're afraid you're not good enough or smart enough or pretty enough or talented enough.

Maybe you've got your eye on a demanding career, but you also want to get married and raise children.

Maybe you're afraid you don't have what it takes to get where you want to be.

I get it. Believe me, I get it.

If I could sit down next to you when you are feeling these aches and pains and wonderings, I'd look at you and tell you the truth.

Your life does not have to be defined by the story you've lived thus far.

It is not limited by what you can and can't see today.

God has beautiful plans for your life that you can discover over time.

Most of all, I want you to hear that you've got this. You can do this.

When I was just starting high school, I was hiding my light. I didn't even know where the switch was to turn it on. You might be there too.

What's most important is that you know it's your responsibility to show up for your life. And as you learn more about who you are and about God's good intentions for your life, you're not only going to show up, but you're also going to kill it.

Beloved, dare to trust that God's desire is for you to live out a beautiful story He designed with you in mind.

Choose to own your story.

Be honest.

Tell the truth.

The good, the bad, and the ugly. Whatever happened, you survived. You are still here.

Own your story.

The girl you want to be is depending on you.

Reflections for the Rescue

REMEMBER

Owning your story is an act of strength.

REFLECT

- Are you comfortable owning your story? Why or why not?
- Do you believe with all your heart that God has given you the power to create a beautiful story when you show up for your life?
- Are you willing to make the effort to discover and embrace the goodness God has for you?

RESPOND

Own your story. Over the next seven days, spend a few minutes each day writing down defining moments in your life's story.

---

2 CORINTHIANS 12:9; PSALM 15:1–2; JOHN 8:32; JEREMIAH 12:3; PSALM 139:1; PSALM 145:18

CHAPTER 2

No One Else Like You

You are a masterpiece

I want to tell you about a teenage girl who might be a little like you or a lot like you. Her name is Kariss.

When Kariss was in sixth grade, she was struggling in school. Academics were difficult. Good grades didn't come easy. Kariss worked really hard to succeed. When she came home from school, she'd grab a snack and start studying at the kitchen table. She even stayed up late studying. And some mornings she'd get up early to prepare for tests. But achieving in academics continued to be a challenge.

Basically, schoolwork was not her jam, but since the law says kids must attend school, she hung in there and did her best.

A friend of Kariss' mom encouraged her to homeschool Kariss. If you're not familiar with homeschooling, it is literally *exactly* what it sounds like. Kariss began learning at home. While some people think that means getting to bake cookies, walk the dog, and play basketball in the driveway all day, kids who are homeschooled are responsible for learning the same content as students in traditional schools. Now you know.

When Kariss finished her core classes each day, she was given time to develop other interests. Kariss wanted to learn how to sew, and her mom pulled out the sewing machine, showed her how it worked, and set her free to create. Kariss was really creative, so her mom found someone who could give Kariss drawing lessons. When she was given the opportunity to explore and discover other parts of who she was, Kariss began to flourish. She was happier because she was being the girl God created her to be.

And I got to see it firsthand, because Kariss is my daughter. (You saw that coming, didn't you?)

Okay, yeah, so I'm a little biased. I think she's amazing.

Today Kariss is married and she's the mom to two young children. She owns her own business photographing celebrities, weddings, family portraits, and pet snakes. She is killing it, professionally. Her home is beautifully decorated in her signature style. Seriously, in any given moment it is Instagram-ready. In her free time—lol, she really doesn't have much free time—she sews amazing clothes for her children.

While there's no way I can take any credit for Kariss' current awesomeness, I do think that one of the reasons she's thriving today is because she had the opportunity to figure out and embrace who she really was. I didn't want her to be a carbon copy of me! The world has plenty of people-pleasing copycats. Everyone is so interested in being the same. More than anything, I wanted for Kariss to be Kariss.

To be comfortable in her own beautiful, glorious, unique, custom-made skin.

Maybe you can relate. If schoolwork comes easily for you, another area might take more effort for you. Maybe you dread running the timed mile in gym class so much that you fake a heart attack at the bus stop in order to miss school. Or perhaps when your art teacher asks everyone in class to sketch an apple, yours looks like it's been run over by an eighteen-wheeler. Or maybe when you had to give a three-minute talk in front of your history class you were so nervous that sweat was dripping from your face and hitting the floor (and the guy in the front row). We've all got something, right? Something at which we don't excel. And don't enjoy. Some are mildly unpleasant, and others feel absolutely death-dealing.

What I wanted for Kariss was what I want for you as well. You might have the kind of wildly creative gifts that God gave to Kariss. Or, like me, you might be more inclined toward academic achievement. And, if we're keeping it real, you might have *no idea* yet what makes you *you*. That's cool. Because together we're going to start noticing both what's inside of you, what God has knit into the fiber of your being, and what's outside of you, all that you're experiencing and discovering. I'm not asking you to have it all figured out yet. I'm just asking you to *notice* what it is that lights your fire.

Maybe you feel a spark of satisfaction when you pick up the newspaper for an elderly neighbor from the curb each morning and deliver it to her doorstep.

Maybe you glow inside when you complete a really, really, really hard calculus problem.

Maybe you feel a warm sense of accomplishment when you cook an amazing creative dinner for your family with flavors that pop and delight.

Maybe your joy is ignited when you pen a poem.

Maybe your happy place is kindled when you reorganize your family's chaotic, dusty, sticky pantry, straightening and ordering and labeling. (Ahhh, the thought of that is making me happy inside right now.)

You are uniquely designed, so the person God created you to be is necessarily different than your sister and your best friend and that girl at school who gets straight A's. And that's the way it should be. So I'm just asking you to begin to notice what it is that makes you *you*. And one of the ways to do that is to notice what lights you up inside.

Thankfully, you don't need to be homeschooled in order to discover the unique masterpiece that God lovingly designed you to be. Although I wasn't homeschooled, I feel like I had the opportunity to entertain a host of possibilities as I was growing up. My parents encouraged me to live with wonder, my teachers gave me the courage to explore, my friends allowed me the chance to play, and my world offered me the opportunity to learn and grow. Fall and spring days were filled with homework, school activities, and play with neighborhood friends. The summer months held visits to my grandparents, slumber parties with cousins, and long, boring days with an occasional trip to the library.

From the vantage point of my childhood, I *could* hope and dream. I had a picture of what I thought my grown-up life might look like. I imagined my future family, my future career, and the future places I'd live. I still have the paper with the names of my twelve kids written on it. I figured I would either be a teacher or a famous actress and that I'd live close to my family but have a second home near the beach.

I figured I would honor those desires when I was old enough. You know, when I was "grown and free." (Who knew that escaping childhood meant giving up naps, free room and board, and summers off?)

Every book I read and every person I met introduced me to more of the world that I could experience. I thought of the people I might one day meet, the places I might one day travel, and things I might one day do. And while I have yet to meet Julia Roberts, explore Australia, or release my own album, I haven't forgotten the thoughts that went through my head before I shifted into adulthood.

My thoughts, dreams, and expectations had room to run. I believed in the idea of a masterpiece.

I've believed that all parts of my life—the good, the bad, and the ugly—could come together in the hands of the person who gave me life. I believed through ups and downs that He knew what He was doing and that He could make something beautiful of my life in His time.

And what I believed for me, I also believe for you. I believe that you are a masterpiece. I believe that God designed you for a special purpose. I believe that all the parts of your life— the good, the bad, and the ugly—can come together in the hands of the person who gave you life. I believe that through the ups and downs God knows what He is doing and that *He is making something beautiful of your life* in His time.

Will you decide to believe it with me?

I know a bazillion reasons can make this beautiful

possibility seem unlikely. When girls at school snub you, or ignore you, or outright harass you, it's hard to believe that you are special. When bad things happen in your home, between family members, it can be difficult to believe that you matter so very deeply to God. When all you want is to be noticed by that *one boy*, and he doesn't even know you're alive, it may be a stretch to imagine that God created you as a marvelous masterpiece. When you just want to fit in, you might not want to be a one-of-a-kind unique soul. And it might be hard to believe that God created everything about you—your brain, your body, your heart, your soul—for a particular purpose. So if you're struggling to believe that who you are is precious and purposeful and altogether lovely, I feel you.

That's why, for today, I'm asking you to trust me. In this moment, I'm asking you to give me the benefit of the doubt. I'm asking you to take my word that you are a unique masterpiece. You are. And we're going to notice different ways that you can figure out just what that means for your life today and for the beautiful, messy, unknowable future that God has planned for you.

When I'm with my women friends, I'll mention the "girl" who's still inside each one of us. And when I say that, I mean that girl who lived with wonder and enthusiasm and possibility—whether she was climbing a tree, or drawing with crayons, or flying a kite, or homeschooling her Barbie dolls. I believe that "that girl"—the carefree girl we were when we were less self-conscious!—can give each one of us clues to who we were designed to be, whether we're fourteen, nineteen, forty-two, or eighty-seven!

I want to challenge you to explore what's possible. Be brave enough to believe that a uniquely beautiful life can be yours. As you notice all the ways that God has uniquely designed you to be who only you can be and to do what only you can do, you honor that girl inside you.

You, my friend, are a work of art. And your life can be beautiful.

As any artist will tell you, the key to creating a wonderful work of art is to be committed to the process. Beautiful creations take time. Sometimes they can be messy. And the artist often wrestles with how to produce a winning representation of what lives in the heart, mind, and soul.

The same is true for you. The key to a beautiful life is to keep going. You must decide not to get hung up or stuck. Don't get bogged down in the mess that comes with making a masterpiece. Choose to commit to the creative process.

> Choose to commit to the *creative process*.

Ephesians 2:10 says, "For we are God's masterpiece. He has created us anew in Christ Jesus, so we can do the good things he planned for us long ago" (NLT).

The girl you want to be—or the girl you aren't sure you

can become—is already a divinely inspired masterpiece. Every day that you live, you have the opportunity to do the work of honoring the plan God has for you.

And I want you to know that you have a friend.

I count it as my mission and privilege to share lessons I learned from my journey in the hopes of saving you a few bumps and bruises along the way.

This is your life. You've got this.

And this is me, your new friend, leaning in close with a smile to tell you this:

You have everything you need to create a life you love.

Reflections for the Rescue

REMEMBER

You are allowed to be both a masterpiece and
a work in progress simultaneously.

REFLECT

- What made you pick up this book? What is
  happening in your life that makes you want to hit
  the reset button?
- Do you believe in the idea of a masterpiece for
  your life? Why or why not?
- Have you ever had a moment when you didn't
  feel like you were being the masterpiece you were
  made to be? What did that moment teach you?

RESPOND

You are a masterpiece. Write down three uniquely
beautiful things about the girl in you.

EPHESIANS 2:10; PSALM 138:8; PSALM 143:5;
JOHN 10:10; JEREMIAH 29:11; GENESIS 1:27–31

CHAPTER 3

Heartbroken at Fifteen

You are okay

I met Vicky when I was fourteen. It was at the beginning of that really fun season when I was starting at the public high school where none of my friends attended.

So, yeah, I needed a friend.

I'd also just "graduated" from the middle school youth group at church, to the senior high group. I'd gone from being top dog—well, as "top dog" as you can be in middle school—to being at the bottom of the social barrel.

As one of the pastor's kids, I sometimes felt like all the adults in church knew who I was and had their eye on me. So the fact that Vicky seemed to want to know me, for *me*, made me like her immediately.

I was watching some of the guys shoot hoops one night at church when Vicky sidled up next to me.

"Hi, I'm Vicky. What's your name?"

Vicky was one of the youth group volunteers, a young adult who spent time with us at youth group, Sunday school, and outside of church. She'd invite some of the girls over to her house, and we'd all hang out in her kitchen eating yummy nachos. Vicky was twenty-five, which of course seemed *super* old to me. And for whatever reason, Vicky took a liking to me. She found ways to be in my space, noticing what I was up to. And she'd encourage me whatever season I was in, whatever I was doing.

When I was fifteen, I started dating a boy. Well, since my dad wouldn't let me "date" at fifteen, we probably called it something else. So even though we didn't go on dates alone, our friends knew we were "together." It was so fun to share all that excitement with Vicky, who was kind of like a much older, wiser sister. After the boy and I had been dating for about four months, he decided that he wasn't quite as excited about me as he'd once been.

I. Was. Heartbroken.

Vicky picked me up one evening after dinner and took me out for a milkshake. As I told her what had happened, her face was compassionate and kind.

"I know it hurts," she reflected to me.

It really did. I think my heart might have been severed in two pieces, inside my chest.

As if she could read my mind, Vicky continued, "I know it feels like your heart won't recover, but I promise you: *you'll be okay.*"

Vicky said the thing I found most difficult to believe during that season: *you'll be okay.* To tell you the truth, if anyone else had said it, I probably wouldn't have believed him or her. But I knew Vicky loved me, and I trusted her.

I still do.

Not only did Vicky get me through my tricky teenage years, but she also walked with me through my tough twenties, my thorny thirties, and now my frustrating forties. She has been a witness to the best and worst stories of my life, and the message she lovingly communicates to me has always been the same: "It's going to be okay. Don't get stuck thinking that this is all there is. It will get better."

When I was fifteen, Vicky didn't offer a trite answer or a quick fix. There was no three-step plan or deep theoretical spiritual conversation.

She simply offered me hope. And somehow, even though her words didn't magically erase my circumstances, they offered calmness as a viable exchange for my crazy emotional rollercoaster ride.

Maybe you're facing your own kind of hardship. Maybe thinking about it overwhelms you mentally or even overpowers you emotionally at times.

At fifteen, the "hard" in my life was a breakup. But the hard part of your life right now might be a difficult relationship with a close friend you've had since kindergarten. Or you might feel like your parents just don't get you. Maybe you're struggling to pass Spanish class. Or perhaps you live daily with anxiety buzzing through your bloodstream, stressing you out and keeping you from enjoying life.

Your hardship might simply be that you can't figure out what comes next.

I want to offer you hope.

It seems a little presumptuous to assume I might be able to speak into your life the way Vicky spoke into my life. But to the extent I can share what I received from her, I want to offer it to you: *you'll be okay.*

Where you are today is not where you have to be forever. You may not want to embrace *where* you are, but it is so incredibly important for you to embrace *who* you are. You get to choose. While you can't control everything in your life, you can do at least one thing: every day you get to choose to honor *you.*

> You may not want to embrace *where* you are, but it is so incredibly important for you to embrace *who* you are.

There will never be another person who will grace the face of this earth like you.

There are people whom only you can love, places that only you can go, and things that only you can do the way that you would do them.

You are a unique creation. No one is like you. And that is exactly what makes you so indescribably precious—and totally okay.

My second order of business on our journey together is to remind you that while you cannot control all of your circumstances, every day you can choose beliefs, attitudes, and actions that honor the best of who you are and who you can become.

If you choose to believe that you are defined only by your disappointments and disasters, you will surrender your role in this world, the role that only you can play.

But if you choose to embrace your journey—even the parts that disappoint you, challenge you, or make you double over from the emotional weight of it all—one day you can look back to see the hard times as a *part* of your life and not the definition of it.

Vicky's offer of hope did not erase what was hard for me; however, she did remind me that the way my life looks today is not the way it will look forever. She asked me to believe, and she reminded me that all I see is not all there is.

And I am asking you to believe.

Believe that your present is not all there is.

Believe that all you see is not all there is. It's just a glimpse.

Today, my friend, this very moment, is just that, only a moment.

Believe that your present is not all there is.

I want you to hold up your head and believe that where you find yourself right now—whether by mistake, choice, someone else's actions, unmet expectations, or even boredom—does not define you.

The mere fact that you are reading these words, breathing in and out, and, therefore, alive indicates that you are worth the work of valuing who you are today and doing the work to discover who you can be tomorrow.

If you're in a season of struggle right now, you might feel as though the energy necessary to excavate yourself from the deep is . . .

Just.

Too.

Much.

But here's the bottom line, and I believe this with all of my heart: You are worth the effort.

If you are breathing, you have life, and the life that God has given to you is one that only you can live. You are the only person with the unique combination of your gifts, talents, abilities, history, and design.

Don't give up, girl. You are worth the work of the rescue.

Fight for your life.

Every day. Get up. Keep going.

You are okay.

Come on, say it with me: "I am okay."

You may have to say this over and over until you believe it, and if that's what it takes, do it.

Saying "I am okay" won't eliminate real problems or pressure, but it will allow you to remind yourself there is hope.

Imagine you and I are sucking down a couple of Reese's peanut butter cup milkshakes, and I am reminding you that you are okay. Your journey is a process, and it might take some time.

Still, get up every day, look at yourself in the mirror, and tell that girl inside you that she is okay. You might have to

get up with tears in your eyes, cries from your lips, or heaviness in your heart, but I want you to choose to believe your life is worth the effort.

Don't stay stuck.

Decide to fight for your life.

And with God's help, choose attitudes and actions that will remind you of this:

You are okay. You're still here. You're still alive. You're worth the rescue.

Reflections for the Rescue

REMEMBER

Where you are today is not where you have to be forever.

REFLECT

- When was the last time you let out an ugly cry? What caused it?
- What difficulties have you feeling buried underneath them?
- Even if there is some darkness in your life right now, there is always light if you will just look for it. What is one thing in your life that is right?

RESPOND

Put this book down and look in a mirror. Go to your bathroom or pull a compact mirror out of your purse. Tell yourself you are okay and smile. Force the smile if you have to.

❧

1 TIMOTHY 6:12; PSALM 30:5; 2 CORINTHIANS 4:17; ROMANS 8:18; 1 PETER 1:6–7; LAMENTATIONS 3:21–24; PSALM 34:17–18; PSALM 40:1–3

CHAPTER 4

Hershey and the Highway

The anatomy of a drift

Message: Drifts happen when we get distracted.

In my late teens I was on a long drive—a three-hour drive, to be exact—headed from one Texas town to another.

I'd filled my car with gas and my purse with a few snacks to make sure that I could complete the trip without stopping to put fuel in my car or my stomach.

The best snack in my purse? Hershey bar with almonds.

I was saving that one for the perfect moment.

When that time came, I reached into my purse and felt around for it, combing every nook and cranny of my bag with the tips of my fingers, expecting at any moment to feel the smooth wrapper underscored by the bumpy goodness held inside.

The bar wasn't in there.

I looked over to the passenger seat and then to the floor below.

There it was.

My Hershey bar was on the floor. Somehow it had fallen out of my purse.

Vexed about the dilemma of the snack being just out of my reach, I could hardly focus on the road. Chocolate. Cravings. Are. Real. My brain went into overdrive trying to figure out how to get to my chocolate without having to stop the car.

That chocolate bar was distracting me.

And my distraction caused me to drift ever so slightly outside the safety of the lane lines.

I felt the rumble strips of the freeway underneath my tires.

Drifts happen because we get distracted. We might be preoccupied by something that isn't good for us, or we might be preoccupied with doing the next thing. For a moment—or in a series of moments—we don't pay close attention to who we are. We cease focusing intently on who we want to be, or maybe we never even get started. We lose awareness, or maybe we never knew that living with awareness is important.

How do you stay on track or get back on track in your life? The same way you stay on the road when you are behind the wheel.

The antidote for distraction is focus, the choice to pay attention and live aware.

The antidote for distraction is *focus*—the choice to pay attention and live *aware.*

I drove a little farther, jolted to attention by the reminder from the rumble strips to stay in my lane.

It wasn't long, however, before I started thinking about that Hershey bar again.

Now, instead of simply being distracted by it, I tried to convince myself that I could reach over and grab it without consequence.

I wanted what I wanted and started strategizing how I could get it without incident.

Drifts continue when we deceive ourselves into thinking things aren't that bad. We drift when we rationalize away the truth and deceive ourselves. After distraction has carried us a little way, our conscience might try to call us back to being sensible. We might even have friends, family, or acquaintances ask us about the changes they've noticed in our actions or attitudes, but we tell ourselves and others that we're not that far off course. We justify. Defend. Vindicate. Or attempt to explain away.

⸎

After a while, I'd rationalized away any thought that opposed reaching for that candy bar.

I was consumed with the right now, the immediate.

While my conscience had tried to warn me, I was no longer bothered by thoughts of danger, lack of safety, or even the accidental loss of my life. Because . . . well, chocolate is worth it, isn't it?! I worked hard at discrediting the voice of reason. I no longer listened. I chose not to respond.

Distraction and deception had worn down my sensitivities.

Drifts persist because we become desensitized. Once we've gone too far for too long, we become less shocked by and less sensitive to the changes that we have allowed. The "every once in a while" becomes our norm. We no longer have an inner argument each time we move farther away from our best self—that girl within us and everything she hopes to be.

And when that girl calls, the one we hoped we could be, we don't listen or respond because we don't think she knows what she's talking about. We don't trust her. We dismiss her. Sometimes we've drifted so far that we don't hear her calling at all.

Let me pause to say that some of you may think I'm blowing all of this out of proportion. I feel you. Had I heard this at your age, from my mom or from my favorite aunt, I would have rolled my eyes and kept doing what I was doing. But I want you to hear that even small drifts matter. Please consider the one-in-sixty rule of navigation. For every degree you are off in your direction now, you will be approximately one mile off sixty miles later.

A small drift left unattended will, over time, make a huge impact on your final destination.

A small drift left *unattended* will, over time, make a huge *impact* on your final destination.

I decided to reach for the Hershey bar.

I took my eyes off the road for just a few seconds, leaned way over to the right, and stretched my arm as far as it would go. I looked like I had major yoga skills.

For a moment, I felt the victory of holding the chocolate bar in my hands. The victory was short-lived, though, because I almost simultaneously felt the rumble strips of the freeway underneath my tires again.

I was losing control and flying off the road. I felt the roughness of uneven ground as the car careened over grass, rocks, and dirt.

Drifts and decisions play a central role in the direction of our lives. While a drift occurs through no clear choice of your own or of someone else's, a decision marks a moment when you participated in picking the route.

Maybe cheating on your chem test seemed like the only way to keep an A in the class, but you regretted it later. Maybe quitting your part-time job seemed like a win, giving you more free time, but then you see the bank account you've been building to go to college at a standstill or even diminishing. Maybe when you and the guy who said he loved you were in the backseat of his car, you were certain that you were making a choice that was right for you, and then discovered after you'd broken up that he'd given you an STD.

Just like drifts, decisions can result in lots of justification and have a numbing effect when we disassociate ourselves from our choices. We might even blame others for the decisions we "had" to make—a mindset that says we are not responsible for our actions.

> You, my dear, have the ability to *choose*.

The good news is that if you are in a drift or are dealing with the result of a decision, there is a remedy. No matter how far or how long you've drifted or how many decisions you've made that turned you around and left you clueless as to how to get back, there is an antidote.

You, my dear, have the ability to choose.

⁓

I sat in the median, stunned.

Let's be honest, I felt like a total idiot.

I mean, who puts their life at risk for a chocolate bar? Apparently me, that's who.

The drift didn't have to happen. I had a choice.

⁓

My friend, you can choose to live aware and to acknowledge

the truth. You have the power to change your course. You can either take action, or you can determine your reaction to the story that has unfolded thus far.

It doesn't matter if you've drifted a little or if you are smack dab in the middle of a ditch. No matter where you are or what you've been through, you still have power. The girl in you still has a chance.

I've known a number of young women in their twenties and thirties who wish they'd avoided the drifts they chose as teens. They drifted either because they didn't know or didn't believe that the work of the teen years is to lay a solid foundation for the rest of their lives. Heavy, right? They didn't intend to drift. They were just distracted by snapping and keeping up with what everyone else was doing on insta. They were distracted by the boys they were dating and the ones they wanted to be dating. They were distracted by friend drama. They were distracted by trying to be liked, trying to be loved. Some were even distracted by their hair (#thestruggleisreal)!

I get it. All those things feel so very pressing in the moment. But I need you to hear the flip side.

What you're choosing now is laying the groundwork for the kind of relationship you'll have with God for the rest of your life. The choices you're making now about your education are going to affect what opportunities you can access in the future. What you're doing with your body today—eating and exercising and sharing it with others—forms habits you'll continue. Even choosing whether you'll invest time into getting to know yourself or just go along with the crowd has a lasting effect on who you're becoming.

That's the point: you are *becoming*. You won't wake up one day and discover that you live in a castle, are married to Prince Charming, run a kingdom, and have no more bad hair days. It doesn't work like that. Today—this day, this very day—you are becoming the woman you'll be in five years, ten years, or fifty years.

And that's the reason drifting matters. Even teeny tiny baby-size drifts away from that girl inside of you—who's been created in the image of God and is growing into an amazing unique woman—are worth noticing.

One second you're eyeballing candy on the floor of the car, and the next thing you know you're in a ditch. I don't say that to scare you. I say it because drifts are preventable. Moment by moment, choose to keep your hands on the wheel and your eyes on the road.

Hang on.

Look ahead.

Stay between the lane lines.

And plan to reach the beautiful destination for which you're headed.

Reflections for the Rescue

REMEMBER

You, my dear, have the ability to choose.

REFLECT

- What are some distractions preventing you from living fully aware?
- How have you rationalized a drift?
- Are you desensitized? What used to bother you that you no longer notice?
- What decisions have you made that have resulted in consequences you are living with now?

RESPOND

Write this affirmation down somewhere
where you will see it and see it often:

I'm still here. I'm still breathing. There must be more.

PHILIPPIANS 3:13–14; 1 PETER 3:10–11; ISAIAH 30:15;
LUKE 5:31–32; 2 CORINTHIANS 7:9–10

CHAPTER 5

Whose Girl?

A chapter from my story

As a teenager, I was a "good girl" by all standards, and I liked it that way. I was smart. A straight-A student and usually the teacher's pet. I was proud to know that I pleased my parents and myself by doing things well. I was also very involved in my church youth group. I participated in most of the opportunities to gather with my girlfriends, serve or at least *pretend* to be serving, and hang out as long as I could. I was a leader. I got things done.

Focused. In charge. Maybe a bit bossy at times. I knew what was important, and I ran hard after those things. So apart from being the pastor's oldest daughter, I also stayed visible because I was always running something.

There is no way I would have believed you if, at that time, you'd told me what my life would be like just a few years later. I was too sure, too confident, too on top of things. And this is exactly why the unfamiliar is surprising. It creeps up. Change happens gradually. We don't see it coming. One day we simply look up and are surprised that we no longer recognize our life or the person we've become.

How do I know this?

Because it happened to me.

Imagine we're in my kitchen making nachos. Just the two of us. It's late in the evening, maybe even close to midnight, because that's when girls share all their secrets. I want to share a chapter from my story with you.

If I'm telling you to be brave enough to tell the truth, it's only right that I go first.

෴

I remember the first time "the boy" held my hand. (Yeah, that boy—the same boy that left me heartbroken.)

We were in a little house that my church had converted into a youth center. We gathered there every Wednesday night with other teens to study God's Word, sing songs, and have fun and fellowship.

I'd heard that he liked me, but I wasn't that interested. Mainly because I wasn't that interested in boys. I was much more interested in making the most of my life and trying to discern, even at a young age, how I wanted to live it.

But I do remember when he held my hand.

It was time to close our time of Bible study with prayer, and, just so that he could hold my hand, he crossed the room.

I was an embarrassed fifteen-year-old girl who was being forced, in front of a room filled with her peers, to acknowledge that there was a boy who liked her, and he wanted everyone else in the room to know.

That first time was not the last. He made it his business

to cross the room and hold my hand every single time we closed in prayer. It became somewhat of a joke, something that was expected.

Week after week, teenagers around the room laughed and giggled while I bit my bottom lip out of embarrassment. It was obvious that I loathed the unsolicited attention.

But I was the nice girl.

I didn't want to be mean, and I didn't want him to feel rejected. I figured that I would have to hold somebody's hand anyway, so why not his?

This went on for months. Then one day, he didn't cross the room.

This weekly action had come to be something that I, as well as everyone else, had come to expect, and the absence of his movement was silently deafening.

Over time, something had changed. I'd gotten accustomed to this boy's attention. As he consistently showed me that he cared, I had gradually let down my guard. The laser beam focus on my own life, goals, and dreams had slowly blurred into the starry-eyed gaze of a teenage girl's what-ifs, maybes, and could-happens.

So the day he chose not to cross the room, I felt a void.

I remember thinking that maybe I ought to give him a chance. I remember thinking that maybe he wasn't as much of an interruption as I'd thought. I remember thinking that he wasn't all that bad and that being good friends probably wouldn't do much to interrupt my life.

The day he stopped holding my hand was the day I got distracted. It was the beginning of drifting out of my own lane and into another.

Motivated and preoccupied by a heightened sense of significance and blinded by the excitement of something different and new, the pursued became the pursuer.

Polite chance interactions became more purposeful as I initiated conversation to let him know there was an interest on my part. I lingered a little longer. Asked more questions. Provided fuller answers. I was truly happy to be his friend, the kind of friend who hopes for more than friendship.

As time went on, our friendship grew and I wanted more. More of the feelings, more of the attention, more of him. Where my energy had previously been focused on what mattered to me for my future, it morphed into a focus on what mattered to me right now. And he was what mattered.

The girl I had been faded into the shadows, bit by bit, day by day.

The thing is, the change in my head and in my heart happened slowly. My mindset, actions, and attitudes shifted incrementally. Little by little, the distraction and excitement of young love threw me off my game, and I lost sight of the girl I'd been committed to becoming.

But I didn't notice it.

I slowly morphed from a self-confident, goal-oriented young woman who had a healthy expectation about her potential into a girl who was desperate for the attention and affection that she'd become accustomed to receiving. I grew more and more attached to this young man who made me laugh and seemed to hold me in high esteem.

Schoolwork got less of my time. My grades slipped. I cared less about being the good girl and more about being *his* girl. Pleasing my parents became secondary to spending time with him, talking to him, and feeling those butterflies of first love. I was less of a leader and more of a bystander. Taking on responsibility of any kind wasn't as fun because it meant I would spend less time hanging with him. The intentional and direction-oriented choices of a driven, motivated teenage girl were reduced to unintentional and involuntary reactions. I lost control as my visibility decreased and the relationship obscured everything.

Even when my parents, youth leaders, or even friends questioned my change in behavior, attitude, and involvement, I failed to notice any cause for concern. How could I hear them when I couldn't even hear the voice of the girl inside me? I had all but silenced the very one whose life I'd been so focused on before.

And if that girl was trying to get my attention, I'd drifted too far away from her to hear her clearly.

⁓

Drifts in life don't last forever. Unintentional living eventually reaches a dead end, and to move in any direction requires a decision or a turn.

Drifts in life don't last forever. Unintentional living eventually reaches a *dead end*.

Something delightful and innocent quickly descended into an emotional and physical rollercoaster ride. I'd become addicted to this guy's approval, overtures, and acceptance. He'd grown accustomed to the reality that I was willing to surrender my own worth to obtain his affection.

You could say I was drunk in love.

And like anyone desperate for that which they have cultivated a craving, I was willing to do whatever it took to get it.

I was no longer drifting. I was making decisions. Poor decisions, to be more specific.

Decisions to disobey my parents and the rules they had set up for my protection.

Choices to ignore the wisdom I'd been taught about protecting and respecting my heart, my mind, and my body.

Actions that did not align with what I believed.

I quickly followed the road that led to what I thought I wanted, even when our relationship took a pause. The farther I went down this road for this boy's affection, the more numb I became to the voice of the girl within who was trying to get my attention and tell me I was headed the wrong way. A vicious cycle repeated in my head and in my heart. The more I silenced, ignored, or debated with the girl inside, the smaller she got and the less I noticed her. Guilt, shame, and self-condemnation grew to fill the place that she left void.

Before my senior year in high school started, I was no longer a virgin. The relationship that had started between two young people in a church youth group with the most innocent of intentions had turned into a full-out disaster.

I hadn't noticed how much I'd gradually shifted away from the strong, determined girl I'd once been. I'd lowered the high standards I'd fiercely held, released many expectations of my life, and no longer cultivated the faith that had sustained me.

My drift had led me to decisions that carried me quickly along in a raging current far beyond my control.

Sometimes we drift.

Drifts happen when we unintentionally move away from who we believe we can be, what we believe we can accomplish, or where we hope our lives will take us. A drift is "the decision you make by not deciding."[1]

Maybe it's that first little white lie to your mom.
Or maybe it's being with a boy, like it was with me.
Maybe it's saying something unkind about an old friend to get a laugh from new ones.
Maybe it's cutting one class. Then two. Then a whole day.
Maybe it's letting a friend with a flask pour a little something extra into your Diet Coke at McDonald's.
Maybe it's lighting up during a backyard "sleepover" at a friend's house.

However, if we pause to examine our drifts and see them for what they are—small relinquishments over time—we realize that we do indeed have the power to change.

While you may feel utterly lost, take comfort in this: Just because you're lost, that doesn't mean you're lifeless. Here's the good news: If there is a way in, there is a way out.

Reflections for the Rescue

REMEMBER

The trip through your own narrative is a trip worth making.

REFLECT

- After hearing some of my story, identify at least one drift in your life. What role did your feelings play in your drifting experience?
- When did this drift happen? Why did it occur?
- Are you in a drift? If you aren't sure, ask a friend.

RESPOND

Take the next step. Be brave enough to be vulnerable. Share a chapter from your story with a trusted friend. If you are not ready for this level of honesty, simply tell a friend that you are working on owning your story—drifts and all. Ask them to pray for you as you do.

JAMES 1:12–16; HEBREWS 2:1;
PROVERBS 4:23; 1 PETER 2:10–11; 1 JOHN 1:6

PART 2

LOOK
AT YOUR
life

CHAPTER 6

"But Who's Chrystal?!"

You are a soul

I was twelve.

I don't recall whether I'd started my period yet, but one thing was for sure, I was totally hormonal.

Walking with passion down the hallway, I made the short trip from the room I shared with my sister to my parents' bedroom door and knocked firmly and heavily. Not waiting for the answer, I turned the knob and stepped inside their room.

I took a deep breath and then filled the air with a heart-rending, guttural cry.

"I don't know who I am!"

My father stopped midway across the room and stared at me blankly.

"What?" he said.

"I don't know who I am!" I repeated with a little less force.

"What do you mean you don't know who you are?" My mother still had one hand up, adjusting an earring.

"I don't know. I just know I don't know who I am!"

I was having a full-blown identity crisis. I teetered on the edge of a crucial search for self, significance, and purpose—a journey of self-discovery that, for some, can last a lifetime.

How do you figure out that girl inside you, where should she be and what should she be doing??

Honey, let me just stop here real quick and set the record straight. We're *all* trying to figure it out.

But let me give you a great starting place: *you are a uniquely and divinely created soul, designed to be filled by a living Spirit that is housed inside of a physical body.* We live in a world that seeks to convince us otherwise. More than ever before, we're bombarded with messages that we are creatures of chance who have no purpose or plan apart from whatever we might happen to figure out on our own. You'll hear this point of view in education, in the media, and even in conversations at the lunch table that seek to strip humanity of the fact that we are special. It sounds like:

"It's been a rough week, let's get wasted tonight. I need it."

"Girl, you better get you some of that. He is so fine! If you don't, I will."

"Tell your mom my parents will be home. It's our senior year! YOLO!"

"Just take it. Slip it in your purse. No one's looking. You deserve it. No one will notice."

"If it feels good, do it."

But the problem with doing whatever feels good is that we *do* have a purpose. We are creatures who have a natural propensity toward spiritual things because we are spiritual beings. You don't *have* a soul; you *are* a soul—a uniquely and divinely created one at that.

You are a soul. You are not a product of random forces that ordered themselves miraculously into the exact arrangement necessary to produce life. You are more than the 37.2 trillion cells that compose what you see when you look in the mirror.[2] You are more than your hair color, the color of your skin, or the shape of your derriere. You exist beyond the physical. You are an invisible, immaterial essence that is more marvelously complex than anyone will ever know.

You are created. You are a divinely inspired work of art. You are made in the image of a living God who didn't dump you on the planet to spend a lifetime lost and without a clue about how to exist well and make your days matter.

When God said, "Let Us make man in Our image, according to Our likeness" (Gen. 1:26 NASB), He gave you priority over other living creatures and forms of life. He designed you for more.

You are a divinely inspired work of art.

You are unique. Your purpose was built into your packaging. When God created you, He made you totally different from any other human being who has lived or will ever live on this earth. Your fingerprints are distinct. Your DNA is not repeated in anyone else.

Everything about your design says that no one is like you.

You are not an accident or an afterthought. You are here and conscious of your existence because Someone had you particularly and purposely in mind when He gave you the gift of life.

You are not an accident or an afterthought.

When I told my parents that I had no idea who I was, I was not considering my special design and the truth that the combination of everything that makes me "me" was something to cherish, to study, to understand, and to celebrate.

My feelings—and hormones—were overruling the fact that I was a fantastic female, rare in creation and never to be repeated again.

So are you.

Most girls and women I know struggle, at some point in their lives, to keep that special design in mind. We get ditched by the boy, fail the test, get yelled at by our moms, snubbed by our friends, disgusted by our acne, ashamed of our bulges, and we are left wondering if we actually matter. When you understand that you are a diamond mine of a physical, emotional, and mental combination that has come together in a one-of-a-kind way, that knowledge can change what you see when you look in the mirror.

I have a cousin named Wynter. While I was writing this

book, Wynter suddenly and unexpectedly passed away. She wasn't just a cousin. She was more than a cousin. In fact, I refer to her as my sister-cousin. One of the things that I have always loved and admired about Wynter is how she consistently showed up for her life in major ways.

Of course, since we've gathered together to say goodbye to Wynter, all of her family and friends have been talking a lot about her. As we've remembered her, told and retold stories from her life, I've been reminded over and over again about how showing up for her life was a *theme* in Wynter's life.

And while, yes, she showed up as an adult, I can clearly see how many of her decisions to show up were made as a teen. She took her studies seriously. She was highly involved in her church. She maximized opportunities to grow. I've even heard Wynter herself say that she should have been a statistic based on the circumstances in which she was raised. Wynter's life wasn't perfect but she worked really hard to make the most of what God had given to her.

Before Wynter passed away, I asked her for her permission to talk about her four daughters in this book because I admired how, as a mom, she was teaching her girls to show up for their lives too. None of her daughters is anything close to being carbon copies of one another—not even the two who are twins! (Girls, I know you're laughing right now because we all know how true this is.)

Alena, who's fourteen is driven to excel in school. She's a writer. And, no joke, she has played a role in a Hollywood movie.

Kaitlyn is eleven. She's incredibly expressive and creative. On any given day, she'll be wearing two wildly mismatched socks, on purpose, and possibly mismatched earrings.

Then there are the twins.

Camryn is calm, straightforward, and knows exactly what she wants when she wants it.

Olivia is creative, theatrical, and truly believes she is starring in a Broadway musical 24/7.

What is so remarkable about these girls, and what is also the win for you and me, is that they have no interest in being anyone other than themselves.

Alena is happy dressing like someone who stepped out of an Old Navy commercial.

Kaitlyn might not ever see her name on the honor roll.

Camryn is fine telling it like it is.

Olivia loves cuddling up next to someone who loves her and never saying a word.

Alena's job and Kaitlyn's job and Camryn's job and Olivia's job is simply to be the best girl they can be.

You too. You don't need to be like anyone else. Sure, recognize and honor what's good in others, but don't sacrifice what's good in you.

You are, first and foremost, a unique soul.

As my tweenage self stood looking at my parents and waited to hear their well-thought-out response, my dad stared intently at me, his eyes full of disbelief and confusion.

And then he laughed.

And then he laughed a little harder.

Once he started, it was as if he didn't have the power to stop.

And I lie not when I tell you that this story is still one

that will occasionally surface during family get-togethers, and my dad laughs just as hard now as he did then.

He laughed because he thought it was comical how difficult I was making a seemingly simple matter.

"What do you mean? You are *Chrystal*!"

His answer was not satisfactory.

"But who is Chrystal?" I asked.

"Oh, my *goodness*."

"I'm serious, Daddy!"

But I couldn't help allowing a slight smile to break through the tears that had just streamed down my face a few seconds before.

"You are Chrystal!" he said with a smile of compassion and understanding. "That's all you need to know."

My crisis of identity was deeply felt but apparently also surprisingly uncomplicated.

I was Chrystal—and a uniquely and divinely created Chrystal at that. For that moment, it was all I needed to know, appreciate, and accept.

Knowing what makes you "you" is a process. The art of communicating that both to yourself and to the world around you can take time to develop, hone, and fine-tune.

It's not so much about *having* the answer as it is about learning the answer.

It's not so much about *having* the answer as it is about *learning* the answer.

One of the women who has embraced and celebrated her uniqueness is tennis player Serena Williams. Although she has been called the world's best female athlete, Serena used to be a girl with all the same wonderings and worries as the rest of us. As a young girl, she was small for her age. When her dad would take her older sister, Venus, to play tennis, Serena would tag along. And of course, as a little pipsqueak, she wasn't as good of a player as her sister. Their father taught them both to play, and Serena's only goal became beating her sister.

Today, Serena has accomplished the goals she set out to accomplish. And to achieve those dreams, she had to ignore the opinions of other people about who she should and shouldn't be. She had to fight the voices in her head that echoed those naysaying voices. In a recent Nike ad, Serena explained, "I've never been the right kind of woman. Oversized and overconfident. Too mean if I don't smile. Too black for my tennis whites. Too motivated for motherhood. But I'm proving, time and time again, there's no wrong way to be a woman."

There's no wrong way to be a woman.

There's no wrong way to be you.

God created every human being with a uniquely designed soul, and that includes you. You have been carefully created. You are not identical to any other person—even if you're an identical twin!

What's so marvelous about the way God chose to make each one of us is that there truly is no wrong way to be you!

Your job is to figure out how to be the best *you* you can be.

Your job is to show up and say, "There's no wrong way to be me." (Yup. You see what I did there #rhymegameisstrong.)

It's impossible to be too big or too small.

Too smiley or not smiley enough.

Too dark or too light.

Too driven or not driven enough.

As you embrace what it means to be uniquely you, you *prove* to the world that there's no wrong way to be the unique person God designed you to be.

Today you are in just the right place to begin the wonderful process of self-discovery. And if all you have today is your name and a statement of belief that you are remarkably uncommon and incredibly distinct, that's all you need to know.

Reflections for the Rescue

REMEMBER

You don't *have* a soul; you *are* a soul—a
uniquely and divinely created one at that.

REFLECT

- How have you been tempted to devalue the
  uniqueness of your soul?
- What keeps you from believing in your value?
- Do you struggle with being patient with yourself?
  Why or why not?

RESPOND

Write your name in the blank below:

I am _____, and I'm a
uniquely and divinely created soul.

Now write that statement somewhere you will
see it often. Write it on your mirror with a dry-
erase marker or lipstick. Jot it on a three-by-five
card and tape it on the dashboard of your car.

GENESIS 2:7; 1 THESSALONIANS 5:23; JEREMIAH 1:5; PSALM
139:13–14; 2 CORINTHIANS 4:16; PSALM 62:1; ISAIAH 43:1

CHAPTER 7

Double Blue Lines

You are loved as you are

Walking down the sidewalk on the college campus, I felt nothing.

Numb.

Void of pain or pressure.

Empty.

Stunned.

Pregnant.

I tried to accept the raw reality of my unexpected situation, but I just couldn't bring myself to do it. I'd started out so well. I'd had a plan and a vision for what I thought I would do with my life, but somewhere along the way I'd lost clarity and focus. That vision of who I was and what I thought could come of my life blurred into an unrecognizable mess.

There was no mistaking that the pregnancy test was positive. I had just seen double blue lines in full twenty-twenty. But that didn't stop me from taking a couple more tests. You know, just to be sure.

Nineteen years old. Second semester of my freshman year in college.

My drifts and decisions had turned into a head-on collision.

My knee-jerk reaction was to share my shocking news with the young man I was sure would help me figure out what to do next. Yes, my high school sweetheart. His athletic scholarship and my academic scholarship had placed us on the same college campus. He was just a short distance away.

I had the pregnancy test in my coat pocket. I didn't know how to tell him. I figured physical evidence would do the trick.

I knew he would be in study hall, so I went and asked him to come to a spot where we could have more privacy.

I pulled the pee stick out of my pocket.

We both just stared at it.

And then came those words that no girl ever wants to hear.

"It's not mine."

Crash.

Impact.

Collision.

I stood there with a blank look and an open mouth. What he was suggesting wasn't even possible.

Then came the feeling of pain, a sensation of pressure, and a flood of thoughts that were fighting to become words I could speak out loud.

None came.

But the tears did.

They forced their way out of my body—hot, fast, and

furious. They flowed and continued to flow like a leaky faucet for days, weeks, and months.

During those difficult days, I can't tell you how many times I wondered how I'd ended up pregnant and alone.

I mean, of course I knew *how* it happened. I just couldn't believe that it had happened to *me*.

My heart had been ripped apart, both by rejection that seemed too much to bear and responsibility that seemed too much to carry.

All I wanted was to pinch myself and wake up from a life I couldn't believe was now mine.

Sometimes collisions happen because over time we drift, unaware, until nothing is left but the impact that shocks us awake.

At other times collisions happen because we stop paying attention to the beauty of our souls and the pulse of our existence. Damage can also happen when we make decisions that have consequences—some foreseeable; some not. Maybe you knew when you entertained a certain someone that it wasn't good for you, but you did it anyway. Maybe you quit playing a sport you used to love and regret it now.

Pay attention to the beauty of your *soul* and the pulse of your *existence*.

Or maybe you got in with a rough crowd of people and now you've lost your sense of direction.

Crash.

Impact.

Collision.

Choices result in outcomes of all shapes and sizes.

Let's face it. Some collisions are our own fault. Warnings all over the place beg us not to text and drive, statistics telling us that it can result in a crash or, worse, death, but people still do it.

Sometimes the responsibility for damage lies with multiple parties, making it difficult to assign blame or figure out where things started to go wrong. At what point did the relationship with your sister become so abrasive? When did your relationship with your mom start to sour? When did the prank that was supposed to be funny turn so destructive?

In other instances, the pain you feel and the brokenness you live with have nothing to do with you. You could be the victim of others' actions.

When the neighbor's son violated you, it affected *your* view of men, and your relationships with them too. When your mother critiqued you, when not even your very best was ever good enough, it caused *you* to feel as if you could never measure up. The cruel words that other kids aimed at you found their mark.

People often ask me what kept me going during that difficult season of my life. They wonder what helped me give birth to my baby, graduate from college, and hold myself together.

It was no walk in the park.

That season was indeed very hard.

But in that place, God met me.

Right there.

The place where my drifts and decisions had led me.

The place where my lack of attention, intention, obedience, and common sense had dumped me.

The place where my soul, while still rare and beautiful, sat isolated, broken, and bruised. Where it seemed no one could reach me to help me, heal me, or guide me home.

He was there.

And I was desperate.

You may have known your own kind of desperation.

If you've been hospitalized for an addiction or eating disorder, you know what desperate feels like.

If you've wanted to harm yourself, you know desperation.

If another's offense against you has left you with emotional wounds that throb when you wake up in the middle of the night, you understand despair.

If, like mine, your life hits a brick wall, that point after which nothing will ever be the same, you understand.

If it feels as though your life is unsalvageable, you *get* what it is to feel desperate.

When I was in that place of desperation, I picked up a Bible, searching for words from God's letter that would affirm my value in His eyes. One by one, I copied down verses that told me what He thought about me. I wrote those words on a piece of notebook paper and carried them around in my pocket, adding more Scriptures here and there as I discovered them.

One piece of paper became two, and then two became three. I stapled them together, folded them up, and carried those precious words with me at all times. Whenever I felt a pang of guilt, shame, or pain, I pulled out those verses and read them until I felt the love of God wash over me. If I found myself unable to control the tears that welled up throughout the day, I'd pull out the paper and read it again and again and again.

In that dark, desolate, damaged place, I learned the value of who I am because of *whose* I am.

> I learned the value of who I am because of *whose* I am.

Whether you attend church regularly or haven't cracked open a Bible since your grandma read it to you when you were five, this is the truth that forms the foundation for everything else in your life:

You are loved.

Your drifts, decisions, and collisions don't define you. So if you feel lost in your life, grab hold of that truth and don't let it go.

You may be reading these words and thinking,

Chrystal, you don't know me. I've already messed up too bad.

I've used hard drugs, and I'm afraid they messed up my brain.

I've been with a lot of guys and I feel dirty.

I've been cutting myself, and I don't think the pain will ever stop.

I've already been kicked out of school.

My mother said she wished I'd never been born.

You might feel like it's too late.

You're too broken.

There's no hope.

I understand. I wish I had a magic wand that could change your circumstances to spare you from the pain you've suffered. And while I know it can sound very trite, I want you to hear this: it doesn't matter.

It doesn't matter.

I don't mean that all you've endured doesn't matter. It matters deeply to God and to me.

I mean that there is nothing, absolutely nothing, in heaven or on earth that can disqualify you from being eligible for God's love.

Right now, wherever you are, whatever you've done, whatever has been done to you, you are worthy of God's love.

Today, you are loved exactly as you are.

If you're like a lot of girls and women, once that unchanging reality enters your ears and eyes, it sometimes takes awhile to make its way into your head and eventually sift down to lodge in your deep places. You've read the words on the page, or you've heard them spoken to you, but they haven't really penetrated the wall of guilt or shame around your heart.

That's okay.

Be gentle with yourself.

Give yourself grace.

Practice patience.

Just because you don't *feel* God's love, in any particular moment, does not cease to make it true.

God loves you.

Right now.

Exactly as you are.

Ironically, or maybe not at all, I didn't understand that truth until I was at my lowest point. When I thought I was successfully pleasing God and everybody else, I didn't need to get it. But when I found myself in the bottom of a dark miry pit, where I couldn't see a way out, I finally understood the height and depth and width and breadth of God's love for me. I understood that, at my best and at my worst, I was loved. God loved me even when I didn't love myself.

As basic as it sounds, those little pieces of notebook paper helped sift God's truth into my deep places. Rehearsing the truth, even though I didn't feel it, gave it more grip.

Maybe today you don't feel like what I'm telling you is true. That's the whole point. You may not. But because it's God's truth, and not mine, I hope you're on your way to believing it. I didn't start receiving it until I was nineteen. So if you're struggling today, I hope that together we can catch it a little earlier. I understand your road may be or may have been a hard one. That's why I want you to know, in your head and your heart and your bones, that nothing you could ever do could separate you from God's unbreakable love for you.

You. Are. Loved.

Believe the loving words from One who went to great lengths to make sure you are the only one of *you* there is. I know that might be a daunting task, especially if you are in a dark and lonely place, so let me get you started with a few truths that have been especially meaningful to me:

- "You are precious and honored in my sight, and . . . I love you" (Isa. 43:4).
- "I have loved you with an everlasting love" (Jer. 31:3).
- "You did not choose me, but I chose you" (John 15:16).

You, my friend, are loved.
Believe it.

Reflections for the Rescue

REMEMBER

You are loved.

REFLECT

- As you were reading, what collision came to mind?
- What consequences are you facing from your past decisions? How have others' decisions impacted you?
- No matter how bad things may be, nothing changes the fact that you are loved. Commit to rehearsing that idea until it sinks in.

RESPOND

Assemble your own list of verses that remind you of your value in God's eyes.

GENESIS 21:17–19; GENESIS 50:20; ISAIAH 41:10; JEREMIAH 31:3; ZEPHANIAH 3:14–17; JOHN 3:16; 2 CORINTHIANS 1:9–11; REVELATION 3:9

CHAPTER 8

Knowing Isn't Growing

Take action

Message: It's not enough to know the right thing, you need to choose it.

You remember the whole Hershey's bar debacle, right? So you know how I am. If there were smart phones when I was a teenager, I totally would have been tempted to take my eyes off the road. But . . . no smart phones. Yet I still found a non-chocolate-related way to endanger my life and the lives of others while driving.

You remember that three-hour drive between two Texas towns? One of those was where my parents lived and one of them was my college. So let's just say I traveled that route frequently.

Before smart phones, there were magazines. (They're a

bunch of glossy papers stapled together with words and pictures printed on them.)

As horrified as I am to admit it today, I would prop open *Seventeen Magazine* on the steering wheel and hold it in place with my left hand. Because I needed to know all the latest make-up tips and stay up to date on the hottest fashions the late '80s had to offer. Peeking quickly at the irresistible pages, I'd grab a sentence or two, and then glance back up at the road.

Listen, y'all, I knew it wasn't the right thing to do.

Obviously, reading a magazine and driving is dumb.

But did that stop me?

Nope.

Because I wasn't willing to pause to compare the value of my life, and the lives of countless others, with the temporary pleasure that was delivering me from boredom.

Showing up for your life means acknowledging that you, my friend, are carrying precious cargo.

You, my friend, have a job to do.

> You, my friend, are carrying *precious cargo.*

Never forget that *you* are behind the wheel. Your choice to live with acute awareness is the key to getting where you've been designed to go.

If we're honest, we do a lot just to pass time.

#Netflix

#Hulu

#Insta

#Snapchat

It's not that there's anything inherently evil about those things, but the distractions we choose do keep us from being fully engaged behind the wheel of our lives.

They distract us from the reality that every moment we've been given is unrepeatable.

Each moment is God-breathed, God-given.

It's probably super-obvious to you that burying my face in a magazine while driving was really a bad choice. And it goes both ways. If I ever drive past you and see you texting and driving . . . well, just don't do it . . . you don't want to see my crazy come out.

Isn't that the way we often operate? It's often easier for us to notice how others are zoning out, staying distracted, and failing to take action, than it is to notice it in ourselves. Human nature, I guess. But getting scolded by someone else isn't usually effective, anyway!

That's why I want you to notice what it is that keeps you from acting on what you know to be true about who you are.

What do you do to pass the time?

What do you do to make life a little less boring?

What do you do to numb out?

Hear me: I don't want you to just identify what's holding you back, and then not do anything about it. That makes as much sense as knowing it's not the greatest idea to read and drive and do it anyway. There's only value in noticing where you need to start taking action and begin moving forward, if you're willing to . . . well . . . move.

Song of Songs 2:15, part of the wisdom literature of the Old Testament, says, "Catch for us the foxes, the little foxes that ruin vineyards, our vineyards that are in bloom." The writer understood that it wasn't just crippling drought or massive flooding that could ruin a harvest. A harvest can be ruined by something small and quick! The things we don't think will harm us. The thieves that seize our fruit when we're not paying attention.

Beloved, your life is worth paying attention to.

You may not make a cataclysmic choice, like dropping out of school or getting a full-face tattoo, that changes your life forever. In fact, more often, it's the little choices and distractions—*that one really important text that I have to send right now*—that can send our lives into a tailspin.

While you may be tired, distracted, or just taking a break from living with focus or resolve, you're not dead. My desire is to call you to attention and beg you to live alert, be responsible, and operate in full awareness of the possibilities that lie within you.

Does God love you? Yes, He does.

Do you have value? Yes, you do.

But if you won't operate on those truths, you're not unleashing their power in your life.

You can't simply read the words of encouragement that I write in this book—or the words inspired by God Himself in the Bible—and merely know them. You must believe them to the point of taking action. Knowledge that does not result in action is simply information.

Just because you know doesn't mean you grow.

The way you think about yourself is the starting point of

renewing your actions. Proverbs 23:7 says, "For as he thinks within himself, so he is" (NASB). How you think affects what you do.

It's one thing to hear and comprehend that God loves you. It's another thing to appreciate and be grateful for that love. But it's a whole 'nother thing to believe that truth enough to receive it, accept it, and then act on it. Your willingness to

Just because you *know* doesn't mean you *grow*.

engage with what you've seen, heard, or understood is what influences the way your life unfolds.

Action based on belief changes you from the inside out.

God did His part by loving you first (1 John 4:19), but you do your part when you choose to receive that love by being rooted and grounded in it (Eph. 3:17) and loving yourself enough to take your precious life seriously.

Yes, God wants to guide and direct you, but He doesn't live through you *apart* from you. He's given you what you need, but you have a role to play and a job to do. You are a recipient of God's grace (Phil. 1:7), but He wants you to respond to His call on your life (Heb. 3:1). You have everything you need to do this because you also share His divine nature (2 Peter 1:4).

You have to participate consistently and intentionally in your life. That's your job.

If you *don't* choose to be alert and attentive, it's easy to drift, make decisions that halt your progress, or even cause a collision. And if you don't value your individuality, you will

It's your job to participate *consistently* and *intentionally* in your life.

find it difficult to see worth in the fragments or debris left after someone has collided with you.

I want to make this as clear as I can.

It is your job in this life to know and value what makes you *you* and to treasure the opportunity you have to make a distinct impression with this one life you have.

No one else can do this for you.

Only you can choose to act as if what you say you believe is true.

Reflections for the Rescue

REMEMBER

You, my friend, are carrying precious cargo.

REFLECT

- Have you been living alertly, responsibly, and fully aware? If so, how do you know? If not, why?
- What are the most tempting distractions for you?
- Are you choosing to act on what God says is true about you?

RESPOND

- Identify your biggest struggle in carrying your cargo well: (1) hearing: "I don't know God's perspective about me," (2) understanding: "I don't know or love my God-given cargo well," (3) believing: "I don't always act as if what I know and understand is true."
- Pinpoint one thing you can do this week to participate intentionally in your life.

ISAIAH 43:4; ISAIAH 49:5; MATTHEW 10:29–31;
LUKE 12:7; PSALM 8:4–5; 1 PETER 2:9

CHAPTER 9

Highlight Reels, Photoshop, and Good Lighting

Comparison can kill

When everyone at my high school was getting asymmetrical haircuts, I got my hair cut in back on a slant. As I walked out of the salon, with every hair falling neatly in place, I felt like I belonged in a Salt-n-Pepa video. (Just trust me on this one, that would have been the ultimate in cool.) I wore a silk cap to bed that night, and the next morning I strutted into school like I owned the place.

A week and a half later, my hair wasn't exactly behaving. I didn't know how to maintain it. So rather than flowing seamlessly in a crisp slant, it just looked like the right side was long and the left side was short. Not at all what I'd been going for. Honestly, I hadn't thought it through. For the style to succeed, it had to fall just right, and a few hairs being out of place would mess that up. Some girls live for that kind of attention to grooming, but I was not one of them. I'm more of a pull-it-into-a-ponytail-and-go kind of girl. So I couldn't wait until that haircut grew out.

Isn't that the way it is? Beforehand, I thought all my problems would be solved if I got that stylish haircut. Joking. Not joking. Suddenly, once I got what everyone else had, I was comparing *my* asymmetrical haircut to *their* asymmetrical haircuts!

Comparison can kill.

Don't take my word for it that comparison is death-dealing: statistics show that, among people who use social media platforms like Insta and Facebook, the people who *post* are, in general, happier than people who just *scroll*. The "scrollers" are those who are just watching other people's "awesome" lives on their feed.

Comparison can *kill*.

Fascinating, right?

Let's imagine that you're grounded, and you're stuck at home, alone, in your room. You're lying on your bed, with your bare feet kicked up on the wall, as you're looking at your phone. So you click open Instagram and start scrollin'.

The first thing that pops up just about does you in. A frenemy posts a glamour selfie at a party she's throwing while her parents are away skiing.

First of all, she looks ah-MAY-zing. Lighting is good. Skin is flawless. Makeup is on *point*. Hair is on *fleek*. Outfit had her looking like a whole snack.

You, on the other hand, are wearing a stained Habitat for Humanity T-shirt and your brother's Batman pajama bottoms.

Frenemy: one. You: zero.

Then you start looking behind her, at her custom-decorated bedroom. You see the speakers that you begged your parents for last Christmas and didn't get.

Glancing around your own room, you make a mental note to lose the papier-mâché fish from first grade, the participation trophy from the fifth-grade spelling bee, and the "World's Greatest Daughter!" birthday card from your corny parents.

Frenemy: two. You: zero.

In the next picture this frenemy posts, you see your ex best friend dancing with the guy you're crushing on.

Enough said.

You get the point.

When we compare ourselves with others, we nurture a lack of respect for our own journey. We look at their lives and construct opinions of them—and ourselves—based on what we see. The problem is we're never operating with full intel.

We don't know someone's whole story. People are really good at editing their lives, leaving out what they don't want to show and spotlighting what they're comfortable revealing. (And even though you *know* your frenemy had to take fourteen selfies before posting the perfect one, that doesn't change the fact that her life *looks* awesome.) We all know that people share more of what's right than what's wrong in their lives. Consequently, we contrast what we can see—much of it edited and online—with our own experiences, comparing the best of others' narratives with the worst of our own stories.

I love this quote by Pastor Steven Furtick: "One reason we struggle with insecurity: we're comparing our behind-the-scenes with everyone else's highlight reel."[3] Now, there is real truth.

When you and I compare ourselves, we engage in an activity that doesn't do anything to help us get where we want to go. We waste energy and emotions on something that takes away from us instead of building us up. When we engage in comparisons, we're fighting a battle we're bound to lose.

❦

There was never a magic moment when I "got over" comparing myself to others. That's just not a realistic expectation. Comparison is something that most of us will continue to deal with in varying degrees throughout our lives. And while we probably can't eradicate it, we can learn strategies that help us flourish by choosing not to play the comparison game.

Let me suggest three practical strategies:

The first one is pretty obvious. Take a break from some of the habits that leave you feeling "less than." If fifteen minutes of scrolling through other people's highlight reels leaves you feeling lousy, just say no. Although the world—and advertisers—will try to convince you that being on social media sites is like breathing oxygen, it's really not the case. Maybe you'll "fast" from social media during the forty days before Easter. Or maybe you'll choose one Saturday each month where you just *enjoy your life*, rather than recording and posting it or obsessing over other people's awesome lives. Maybe you'll decide to shut it down two hours before bedtime each night. I encourage you to give it a try, in some form or fashion, and notice what taking a break does for your insides.

The second practice is a little sneakier. No, it's downright subversive! You know that feeling when you pass one of the most popular girls in school in the hallway and she looks like she just stepped off the red carpet during BeautyconLA? It's that feeling that can make you feel small. Although it's counterintuitive, the antidote is to behave like the bigger person. Don't worry, that doesn't mean that you put the girl down or make her feel small. Actually, it's just the opposite. When you gather your nerve to offer this girl a compliment—remarking about her unusual jewelry or a unique scarf—you break the power that comparison has over you. I know it sounds unlikely, so please do me a favor and just try it, will you? I have a lot of confidence that it'll be a big win.

It's not hard, either.

"Hey, it looks like you had a great time in Hawaii. So cool that you saw a baby shark!"

"Ooh, that hat really makes the color of your eyes pop."

"I heard you broke your record in the 400 at the meet yesterday. So proud of you!"

"The prom-posal you posted was so sweet. I hope you have an awesome time at the dance."

Can you feel, in your body, how complimenting others becomes not just a win for them, but a win for you too?

Finally, when you receive a compliment, I want you to accept it. Because the cousin of allowing other people's "big" to make you feel "small" is actually making yourself smaller by rejecting compliments.

Think about it, what *do* you typically say when others offer positive comments?

"Aww, it's no big deal."

"Well, I didn't do as well as I would have liked to."

"It's not as pretty as yours."

"But I'm not as talented as . . ."

Stop!

When someone compliments you, receive it! Say two words: "Thank you."

Sometimes we fear that simply acknowledging that which shines in us or saying thank you makes us stuck up. Or full of ourselves. Or arrogant. Or conceited. Or . . .

Nope. It only makes us gracious. So practice receiving the kind words that others offer you.

Comparison is a habit. That means you can choose not to practice it. Nothing is good about practicing an activity that only results in feelings of competition, envy, or strife. The good news is that you have everything it takes to break the death grip of comparing yourself to others.

Comparison is a *habit.* That means you can *choose* not to practice it.

Take a break from habits that cultivate comparison.

Be bold and compliment those whom you might otherwise envy.

Receive the kindness others offer you.

You know that only one person's opinion of you matters, right? And that person is *not you*. It's not the guy you want to be dating. It's not your archenemy. It's not even your best friend. While we sometimes let the opinion of others bully us, ultimately the opinion that matters is that of the One who made us. So take the time to figure out what the girl in you desires and what God desires for her too. Act as if only one standing ovation matters for the way you live.

God will not ask you about how you lived in comparison with other people. He will only want to know that you did what you could with what you had, trusting Him for the progress and *the* answer only He can provide. After all, He made you.

ॐ

Take the energy and emotion you would spend thinking about what other people have or are doing, and instead spend that time and energy being grateful for what you have and can do today. When you focus on what's right in your world, you limit the power of what's wrong to steal your joy. The more you see what's beautiful in your life, the less what's outside your life will matter.

Gratitude is going to help you stay grounded in what is most real and most true. Gratitude is the practice of being thankful and showing appreciation. Write what you're thankful for on sticky notes and post them inside your locker, on your bedroom door, tape to your bicycle, or inside your family's refrigerator.

Gratitude for your own circumstances and accomplishments also frees you to appreciate the accomplishments of others.

Listen, my friend. Whatever photo-shopped, filtered, highlight reel others are posting has nothing to do with you. I hope you hear that as a word of freedom. No one is like you, either in years gone by or in years to come, who will have your exact smile, sparkle, wit, insight, or purpose.

Freedom comes when you stop comparing yourself with the girl who has more privileges, more opportunities, more followers, and more likes.

Take a break from habits that drag you into the dark place and stop letting other people's touched-up glamour shots be the boss of you.

Be generous in building up others.

Receive the kindness others offer you.

As you embrace the reality that nothing about you is "less than" or "more than" others, you will be free to live exactly how you were made.

Reflections for the Rescue

REMEMBER

God will not ask you about how you lived
in comparison with other people.

REFLECT

- Whom do you typically compare yourself with?
  Name a person or simply a type of person (pretty,
  smart, fit, spiritual, etc.).
- In what areas of your life are you most envious of
  others?
- Take a moment to practice contentment. What's
  right in your life? What's good about your life
  today?

RESPOND

Knowing that you are ultimately living for an
audience of one, what are your benchmarks?
What do *you* want to achieve? Who do *you* want
to be? What does God require of you?

PHILIPPIANS 4:11–13; LUKE 12:15; MATTHEW
6:25–26; HEBREWS 13:5; 1 TIMOTHY 6:6–7;
PROVERBS 28:6; ECCLESIASTES 3:13

CHAPTER 10

Just Say No to Dr. Pepper

Participate in the process

Every day before high school track practice I'd stop by the beverage vending machine, drop my quarters into the coin slot, make my choice, and wait for the satisfying clunking sound of a can of cold Dr. Pepper magically appearing at knee-level. Then I'd dig into the bottom of my purse and find more change to drop into the snack machine. I pushed the button labeled E6 and watched as the circular wire barrier twisted backwards to release what I told myself was "fuel" my body needed: a pair of Reese's peanut butter cups. (Protein, y'all. Strong bodies need *protein*.) So basically, my athletic life was powered by the holy trifecta of caffeine, sugar, and fat.

At sixteen, running track, I could pound a lot of junk food without my body showing unsightly bulges of weight gain.

Being sixteen was *awesome*.

In a lot of ways, being a grown woman is also awesome. But I won't lie: the minivan of life does not lend itself to Dr. Pepper and Reese's. Do I enjoy the occasional indulgence? Heck, yeah. Do I notice extra padding in my middle when I overindulge? Absolutely.

The habits you're developing today have consequences. The choices you make now in all kinds of areas create a trajectory that determines what your life looks like in the future.

Physically, the food you eat and exercise you perform are going to develop a body that you either love later or will need extra care because you've been unkind to it.

We can think about our bodies in two ways: how they appear and how they function.

Much of our culture—the images we view online, the actresses who star in our favorite shows and movies, the photographs of models in magazines and on billboards— esteems physically attractive bodies. If I were to ask you what the ideal beauty standards are for women and girls, I am certain that you could quickly rattle off what kind of hair, eyes, skin, lips, arms, abs, butts, and legs our culture values. Whether anyone ever named them explicitly, you've naturally picked up on what men and women like.

A second way to value bodies is by how they function. By that I mean that we might choose to value eyes that notice others, arms that serve, and laps that toddlers can crawl up into for stories before bedtime. (They love a soft lap. So, to my kids and grandkids, *you are welcome*.) I watch my friends with physical disabilities bless others with their faces, call out to others using their vocal chords, and give hugs generously. God gave us bodies as a way to be in relationship with others, with Him, and with ourselves.

Your body is the literal physical vessel you use to fulfill God's unique plan and purpose for your life. And because you get just one, it's got to last a good long while.

Elisabeth Elliot said, "Discipline, for the Christian, begins with the body. We have only one. It is this body that is the primary material given to us for sacrifice. . . . We cannot give our hearts to God and keep our bodies for ourselves."[4]

It is true that your body is temporary. It is not designed to last forever. Each and every day, your body moves one step closer toward its inevitable end. So it stands to reason that if you care about your soul, you should care about the body that carries your soul around.

Plain English?

You have to take care of yourself.

If you are sick and have health challenges beyond your control, I know how frustrating it can be to have physical limitations—especially when your mind and heart yearn to do more than what your body will allow.

But even with physical disability and chronic illness, you still can choose to give yourself the best opportunity to live at *your* physical capacity and release the full strength of what's inside you.

God has called you to care for your outsides, the physical body with which you've been gifted, and to care for your insides.

You are a soul who functions in a spiritual way, designed to be fully alive only when you are overflowing with life that bubbles up with the Spirit of God. And you have the power of the God of all yesterdays, today, and forever who is willing to help you. Just like the power of the engine in your car, the power of the God's Spirit is available to you. But here's the rub: it's up to you whether you are *filled* with the Holy Spirit.

To be filled with the Spirit, you must regularly invite God into your life by flooding your mind and thoughts with God's perspective—a perspective He makes clear in His Word. You invite God in when you pray, talking and listening to Him throughout your day. You invite God's power in when you allow Him to show you what He wants you to do with the precious cargo He gave you.

Some years ago, a mentor advised me to get up every morning, stretch my hands to heaven before my feet hit the floor, and offer God my mind, my heart, and my day. I still do this often.

But I have to tell you that I struggle with consistency. As much as I want to stay awake and alert to the value of my life, my tendency is to get lulled to sleep, to take breaks, and to forget. So recently, I've decided to be tactical about this.

I've put a reminder on my phone to check in with God on a daily basis. My phone chimes every morning with a message that reads, "Ask God what He wants me to do today." I have this prayer typed in the reminder as a note: "Lord, today I surrender my will to Your way. Help me to be an instrument of Your grace, love, mercy, and power."

As a child, your parents may have been faithful about bringing you to church and Sunday school every week. Or perhaps that wasn't a part of your family's routine. Either way, you're at an age when it's time for you to take responsibility

for you. Cultivating your spirit, ensuring that it's nurtured and fed and strengthened, is up to you.

When we practice sloppy habits, with our bodies or with our spirits, we will eventually suffer the consequences. Maybe not today. Maybe not tomorrow. We might not even notice the ill effects for years to come. But both physically and spiritually, *we are what we eat.*

If you and I were to walk in the front door of my home and beeline for the kitchen, we could open the refrigerator door and find a handful of miniature Reese's cups in there. I still love them. But instead of being the melt-in-your-mouth full-size package of my youth, today I often settle for one single miniature candy cup. And by one, I mean two. I still enjoy the same treats, I just enjoy a smaller amount. The habits I developed as a teen have contributed to the challenge I face now to stay at a healthy weight.

If you're fourteen or fifteen or even eighteen, you might not be feeling the urgency of caring for your body or caring for your spirit. I know that season finale of your favorite show or whether your best friend kisses the guy she just started seeing is much more enticing than self-care. And, if I'm honest, that doesn't always change as you get older! But if you put off those good choices, promising God you'll get to them later, you're failing to participate in the process of who you're becoming.

The process of your life starts now. Actually, it started the day you were born, and this is the season when your parents begin to release their grip on the steering wheel and turn it over to you.

Because my dad was a pastor, my mom took my siblings

and me to church. We went to worship, Sunday school, and youth group. We read, studied, and memorized passages from the Bible. We prayed the prayers and sang the songs and bought the CDs.

It was the same with our physical nutrition. My parents made sure we didn't go hungry and offered healthy food every day. (The vending machines weren't their idea. That was all me.) But today I wish I'd spent more time developing healthier physical and spiritual habits. I've learned that these habits are like any other kind of disciplined training: the earlier you get started, the farther you get. And—I am speaking from experience—you will have less ground to reclaim a few years down the road.

Showing up for your life is not something that happens in the future. It is happening right now. So start honoring the body and spirit with choices that are going to carry you into young adulthood and eventually into old adulthood.

I'm not asking you to start with a marathon. Lord knows I wouldn't wish that on my worst enemy! No, I'm inviting you to take baby steps. Create habits that will grow and develop with you. You can find a devotional guide for teenage girls at your local bookstore, Wal-Mart, or online. Choose one with short entries. Cultivate the habit of reading it every day. Just like you feed your body, feed your spirit. God has written a love letter to you, and it's available to you!

Don't wait until you're twenty or thirty to hear all God longs to speak to your heart.

Start now.

Start small.

Do the same with your body. If you're addicted to

Mountain Dew or McDonald's fries or gummy worms, cut back on your consumption. If you always take the escalator at the mall, start climbing the stairs. Today, start honoring the physical house God has given you.

Living well is your responsibility—to God and to yourself. God is not going to make you play a starring role in your own life. You have to show up and do your part.

You have to participate in the process of who you are becoming.

Reflections for the Rescue

REMEMBER

Staying awake to your life requires your participation.

REFLECT

- On a scale of 1 to 10, how would you rate the care that you give your body? Can you do better?
- Is the Spirit of God operating in your life? How do you know?
- What do you do to invite God into your life? How do you connect with His perspective and power?

RESPOND

Identify two habits—one spiritual and one physical—you would like to be more consistent in. Ask someone who loves you to hold you accountable to doing so.

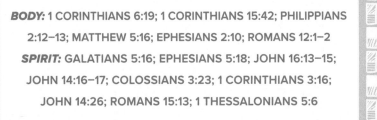

BODY: 1 CORINTHIANS 6:19; 1 CORINTHIANS 15:42; PHILIPPIANS 2:12–13; MATTHEW 5:16; EPHESIANS 2:10; ROMANS 12:1–2
SPIRIT: GALATIANS 5:16; EPHESIANS 5:18; JOHN 16:13–15; JOHN 14:16–17; COLOSSIANS 3:23; 1 CORINTHIANS 3:16; JOHN 14:26; ROMANS 15:13; 1 THESSALONIANS 5:6

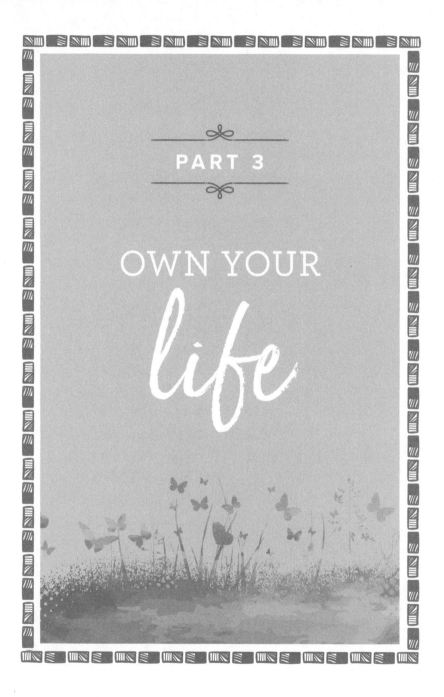

PART 3

OWN YOUR

life

Do What the Ants Do, and Follow the Crumbs

You can know something

One of the rules at the summer camp I attended as a girl was: NO FOOD IN THE CABINS. And like all the best rules, there was good reason for it. That good reason was called "ants." Camp staff had learned the hard way that those sneaky little devils would sniff out crackers, cookies, granola bars, and gummy bears. They'd follow the tiniest trace of a crumb straight to the source, and then call all their friends to line up, file in, capture the booty, and file back out into ant land. But the problem was that they'd keep coming back to girl land, in search of more treasure.

Did I still stash granola bars, my beloved Reese's cups, Capri Sun juice pouches, chips, and Oreos under my bunk? You know I did, girl. And sure enough, those ants did what ants do: they followed the crumbs that were right in front of them and found my stash.

That crumb trail lesson was also a key plot element in the German fairytale captured by the Brothers Grimm. What I'd remembered as a harmless childhood story, upon adult inspection, turns out to be a pretty gruesome tale of child neglect, abuse, and cannibalism. When their parents try to abandon siblings Hansel and Gretel in the woods, the kids catch on to the plan. So that savvy Hansel leaves a trail of white pebbles, and later bread crumbs, in order to find their way home to the parents who tried to do them in. Like I said, *disturbing*.

The contrast of trails related to unwanted insects and child endangerment is the kind of trail that leads you where you want to be. It's the "ladder" square on the Chutes and Ladders board. It's the "Advance to Go and collect $200" Chance card in Monopoly. It's the "Gumdrop Pass" square on the Candy Land game board.

And God is leaving you bread crumbs.

God wants you to notice those clues as you become the woman who knows and fulfills her unique purpose.

God leaves crumbs because He is gracious. It's true, and it's a good thing. These crumbs are signs of His guidance. It's in His nature to do so. Psalm 37:23 says, "The LORD directs the steps of the godly. He delights in every detail of their lives" (NLT).

God enjoys seeing us in the details of our lives, and He helps us on the way by leaving a trail of crumbs right in plain sight.

The first and most obvious of those crumbs are the words that He has taken care, over thousands of years, to make available for our instruction. Psalm 119:133 says, "Direct my footsteps according to your word; let no sin rule over me."

Let me be clear here. Many of the places where I have felt the most lost came as a result of my choice not to follow the trail He had already made clear. I am so thankful that working my way back from the drifts, decisions, or collisions wasn't a guessing game. It simply started with knowing and acting on the words God shared in His letter of love.

⁓

We can't see our path, my friend, if we don't look in *two* places—what God has said in His Word for revelation to all and what He has placed in us individually that directs our lives according to our gifts, abilities, interests, and natures.

Now, I don't mean to sound all super spiritual here. Trust me. During many seasons of my life, I wish I'd been more spiritually minded and more consistent in acting on the principles I'm sharing with you here. But that's what I love about God. He keeps on loving and leading me even when I haven't always been faithful.

He is always loving and leading you too.

Just follow the crumbs.

One of the things I love about the story of Moses in the Bible is that, in hindsight, it's very clear how God led Moses to the place of leading God's people, the Israelites.

In Exodus 2, we read about Moses and his passion for the Hebrew people. Even though he was raised as Egyptian royalty, Moses was so passionate that he murdered an Egyptian who whipped a Hebrew slave.

After running for fear of his life into the desert, Moses no longer had a life of royalty but instead took on the lowly position of a shepherd. He led sheep. Moses learned in exile how to take care of animals that aren't known for being the sharpest tacks. He got practice caring for those who needed constant guidance and direction.

So when God shows up in the burning bush in Exodus 3 and tells Moses it's time to lead the Hebrew people into freedom, Moses is confused. How could God be asking him to do such a thing when he was such a sinful, simple, unsophisticated soul?

God saw what Moses didn't.

He saw Moses' passion and personality as well as the profession he had developed. And God could use those.

Can't you see it?

I'm guessing that it's easier for you to see it with Moses' story than it is to see it with your own. That's the problem, isn't it? It's always so easy to see the trail of bread crumbs in someone else's life.

God will never leave you without a next step.

Right now, in this moment, you might feel like you have absolutely no idea where you are or where you're headed.

That's okay! *You* are okay, remember?

God will never leave you without a next step.

Hints.

Evidence.

Bread crumbs.

This is such good news if you've never had a clear vision of who you wanted the girl inside you to be. You serve a God who knows you better than you know yourself. And He wants to surprise you with who He *knows* you can be!

Let me give you an example.

In the second grade, I found myself in the middle of an effort to bring world peace to the school playground and do my part to break up a catfight between two girls from my class. Nobody asked for my help, but something in my DNA doesn't like to see unnecessary anguish, anger, or heartache. I recall feeling as if it were my duty to help them make peace because if they had peace, then our class would have peace, and we'd have a better classroom. Simple enough, right? In my second-grade brain, it totally made sense that I would spend part of recess with one girl on one end of the playground hearing her side of the story, then walk to the other end to do the same with the other girl.

Fast-forward to high school, where in the church youth group I always seemed to have ideas for how we could make things better and experience more community. I felt like it was my duty to meet with the leaders of the youth group, present my thoughts, and then help implement everything I'd presented. My goal was to create a collective experience that would benefit everybody.

As I look back, the trail is clear. It's easy to see our own crumbs in hindsight.

I love seeing where people are not together and then creating an environment, a structure, or a program to bring them into community.

It's no surprise that today I'm involved in various areas of the women's ministry at my church and am always on the lookout for creative ways to bring women together for the betterment of the whole. Even when no one is looking for my help or suggestions, I can't help but offer them.

Not only is it a natural gift for me but being a gatherer of people is also an ability I've cultivated over time, even without being aware of it. I am passionate about seeing people connect, and because personality tests tell me I'm a perfect balance between an extrovert and an introvert, I am suited for dealing with groups of people while also being a lover of one-on-one.

Back when I was having that identity crisis at age twelve and crying my eyeballs out in my parents' bedroom, I had no idea that creating community is what I'd one day be doing. But it totally makes sense *now*. How did I get there? I followed the crumbs, discovered the knowledge of how God made me, and acted on the opportunities He provided.

⁓

Can I give you one more example of how to make peace with following the bread crumbs?

My sister Priscilla teaches the Bible.

When she was in college, Priscilla worked at a radio station. And because of her familiar voice over the airwaves, someone asked her to lead a Bible study for a group of girls.

She didn't want to do it.

Leading a Bible study was not on her list of things to do. However, she loved God, loved the Bible, and loved to talk.

So she followed the bread crumbs.

She decided it couldn't hurt to lead the study for a while and, well, you probably know how things ended up. (If you don't, just Google "Priscilla Shirer.")

Do you see how this works?

First, you take the time to look at what is inside of you and who you already know yourself to be. Then it's up to you to pay attention to the opportunities that come your way.

And then you act.

Your life's work is to discover and use your unique combination of gifts, abilities, interests, and nature—especially in the spaces and places that are lifegiving for you. In your job, in your home, within your community, and in your church.

You may not know everything there is to know, but you don't have to.

Connect what you know with what you do and watch new trails form in front of you.

Here's what I know.

God is sovereign. He always has a plan and destination in mind.

We just have to follow the bread crumbs.

Or crushed peanut butter crackers.

Or granola bar crumbles.

Follow 'em.

Connect what you *know* with what you *do* and watch *new trails* form in front of you.

Reflections for the Rescue

REMEMBER

You may not know everything there is
to know, but you don't have to.

REFLECT

- What crumbs point to your design?
- What crumbs has God given you in His Word?
  Are you following them?
- What crumbs has God allowed in your
  experiences? What information do they give you?

RESPOND

Name one small step you can take based
on the crumbs you've noticed.

HEBREWS 13:20–21; PROVERBS 16:9;
PSALM 16:11; PSALM 25:4; PSALM 25:10;
PROVERBS 3:6; ZECHARIAH 4:10; PSALM 119:133

CHAPTER 12

The Most Natural Expression of Who You Are

Noticing the gifts God has given

Martha, a friend of mine, is a gifted artist. She can paint huge worship banners without blinking an eye. She can design and stitch together the most colorful clothing without a pattern. And she can create beautiful shareable memes with her hands tied behind her back. Okay, well, maybe she needs her hands.

When Martha looks back at her childhood, plenty of clues signaled that God had endowed her with creative gifts.

Her mother says that instead of asking for new toys, Martha would dig items out of the trash and create new things with the cardboard and plastic she found there.

When her church youth group produced and performed a musical, Martha painted a backdrop that stretched the width of the church sanctuary.

When she was fifteen, Martha entered a pencil drawing of her brother skiing into a local contest and won the prize of private art lessons.

As a high school junior, Martha had only one extra course spot in her senior year schedule. She thought she should take AP physics, but what she really wanted to take was an art class. In an announcement that knocked Martha's socks off, her mother—who recognized the gift God had given Martha—gave her blessing to the art class. Martha was blown away.

Taking the physics class would have looked much more impressive on college applications. But without even realizing it at the time, Martha was actually taking a baby step toward the future purpose God had for her life.

Have you ever taken the time to think about—and maybe even document—the God-given contents you're carrying? God expects us to discover, develop, and deploy our gifts as we live this life. While God gives us life, we honor Him by using what He's placed inside us. We show appreciation when we develop our abilities and skills. We live fully when we make room for our interests and passions. And we gain clarity when we take stock of our nature—our personality, character, and temperament.

God expects us to *discover, develop*, and *deploy* our gifts as we live this life.

The problem is we get busy living and forget to *look* at the life He's given us.

Soon after I quit my first job out of college, I made the time to look, mostly out of disappointment and frustration. The exercise was not very refined, but it was real. I'd decided to pay attention, listen to my life, and gain a fresh perspective on what God had put in me.

I started out listing my gifts. I brainstormed my strengths, areas I was naturally good at. I thought about activities that came easily to me. I knew I was a good listener and a strategic planner. I loved solving problems and figuring things out. Organizing information or people always seemed to be a piece of cake, and words, well, I loved words and had a knack for using them.

What about you? What comes easily or naturally to you that does not come easily for others?

I mentioned that one of the special gifts God has given me is a desire and leaning toward bringing people together. Yes, I like for people to get along, but there's more to it than that. As one of only a few black girls at a private Christian elementary school, I knew what it felt like to not quite fit in.

A girl with another gift, maybe the gift of getting fired up about justice issues, might have spoken out about the need for racial reconciliation.

A girl with the gift of writing may have chronicled her experience and shared it in the school newspaper.

I'm pretty sure you can imagine what this girl did. I purposed to look people in the eyes, people who were easy to notice *and* people who were often overlooked, to let them know that I saw them.

Today that's what I love to do with my online ministry. I gather women together in a space where they can speak, listen, learn, and grow. The heart of the message God has given me to share is that every woman deserves to be seen, heard, valued, and known. I want every girl and woman to know that she—know that *you*—matter deeply.

As a girl trying to find her way in elementary and middle school, and even as a girl who was exercising her gifts as a teenager, I had no way of knowing where the trajectory of my gifts would one day lead.

A gift is something that is a relatively natural expression of who you are. Yes, you can often develop that gift by pursuing education or training to sharpen it. Martha could have graduated from high school and gone to design school. I could have pursued a degree in private counseling. But the essence of a gift is that it's how God has naturally designed you. Each one of us was designed to be seen, known, and loved. And when I use the gift God has given me, I am using that gift for the good of His kingdom.

Sometimes I'll ask a girlfriend how she's doing, and she'll muster up what she believes to be a convincing, "Fine." But you know what? Because my gift is seeing—paying attention to the person in front of me—I can usually see right through her false "fine" and know that she's actually *not* fine. And even if that girlfriend had planned to hide, we usually end up uncovering what's under there, which allows *her* to deal with what's really going on.

And while my girlfriends and other women to whom I minister usually appreciate this gift of "seeing," any of my children who have ever tried to tell me a lie—not mentioning any names—aren't as delighted when my sixth sense kicks in and their falsehood is exposed. (#MomSuperpower)

The variety of gifts that God gives are endless.

Some girls hear music in their heads that they are able to put down onto paper or perform in front of an audience.

Some girls are naturally gifted at academics.
Some girls are naturally faithful and devoted friends.
Some girls are keen observers.
Some girls, who are naturally extroverted, are the life of the party.
Some girls, more naturally introverted, can describe special characteristics about every person in their homeroom.
Some girls have a special eye and heart for those on the world's margins.
Some girls are gifted at speaking in public.

Begin to notice what you're naturally built for. This is part of the work of your teenage life.

I know, I know, I'm commissioning you to work in a lot of areas. I'm not worried you're going to get overwhelmed or burnt out, because mostly I'm asking you to keep your eyes open. To notice.

I'm asking you to show up for your life.

As you think about the broad spectrum of gifts that God gives, notice the bread crumbs.

If you were a thoughtful six-year-old who decorated the house for your mom's birthday, that's a bread crumb.

If, from the first moment you touched a basketball, you

delighted in practicing dribbling, shooting 100 free throws every evening, and running your own line drills in the driveway, that's a bread crumb.

If you hosted your own radio show as an eight-year-old, inviting special guests from the neighborhood and recording it with your dad's phone, that's a bread crumb.

If you snuck out of the house to feed the stray neighborhood cats, even though your mom told you not to, that's a bread crumb.

If you decided to go door-to-door asking neighbors to donate money to folks on the other side of the planet whose homes were destroyed by a natural disaster, that's a bread crumb.

If you stay up late at night, huddled under your covers with a flashlight and a notebook, writing poetry, that's a bread crumb.

As you start to follow those bread crumbs pointing to your natural gifts, you'll be walking the ant trail toward the good purpose for which you were made.

One of my greatest passions is encouraging women and girls to be all that God designed them/you/us to be. In a previous book I wrote, called *She's Still There,* I ask women who are a decade, or several decades, older than you to look back and notice the bread crumbs in their lives. I want them to do a 180 so that they can see that bread crumb of interest they had in third grade, and the bread crumb of passion they had in eighth grade, and the bread crumb of success they had in college, and the bread crumb of joy they had in their first full-time job.

Yeah, I do like to make everyone work hard.

What's so cool is that you, right now, have the privilege of noticing these bread crumbs one at a time. You don't even need a time machine, because they're happening right now. Your youth group leader sees that you have a lot to say and invites you to give a talk to the youth group. You win the state championship in the 100-meter dash. You submit an article to your favorite teen magazine that gets published. You raise money to launch an urban garden that produces fresh produce for local folks who are hungry.

You don't have to look backwards to see the gifts God has put in you, all you need to do is open your eyes.

Today.

Reflections for the Rescue

REMEMBER

The gifts God has given you offer clues
about who you are made to be.

REFLECT

- God has given you unique gifts. What comes
  naturally to you that does not come naturally to
  others?
- What are the bread crumbs you are noticing that
  point to your unique gifts?
- Your history offers clues to your gifts. When you
  look back six or eight years, what gifts were you
  using then?

RESPOND

Ask the people who know you best what your gifts
are. Write them all down and notice any themes
or patterns that might be woven throughout.

❧

ROMANS 12:6–8; 1 CORINTHIANS 12:4; 1 CORINTHIANS
12:11; 2 CORINTHIANS 12:7–11; 1 PETER 4:10–11

CHAPTER 13

You've Learned How to Do This

Cultivating your abilities

In high school, my school hosted a contest in which students were required to demonstrate proficiency in both math and writing.

I know, you might be saying, "Wait, writing *about* math? That just sounds like a cruel form of torture . . ."

First, we took a math test to evaluate our application of concepts, and then we submitted a written paper. The lengthy essay was to be titled: "The Importance of Economics in Everyday Life."

Yeah, right now you're either yawning or, if you're like me, you're already outlining your own essay and Googling who you can submit it to.

I haven't gotten to the best part.

Two winners of the contest would be awarded a trip to the Stock Exchange in New York City.

Yes, *the* New York City.

I'm delighted to report that I was selected as one of the two lucky students. (Insert fireworks emoji here.)

Wait—it wasn't "luck," though, was it? Let me try again . . .

I'm delighted to report that I was selected as one of the two naturally gifted students.

Getting, closer, but not quite there yet . . .

I'm delighted to report that I was selected as one of the two students whose abilities were recognized.

Ahh . . . there it is.

First of all, no "luck" was involved. I worked hard to study for that test and compose that essay. (*Before* there was spell-check, y'all! Early 1990s spellcheck was called "my mom.")

Second of all, although my "gifts" were involved to a degree, since I did have academic aptitude in both writing and mathematics, the competition didn't depend solely on natural gifts.

Let me be plain: I had worked hard to learn all I'd learned to that point.

Yes, God had knit those natural gifts into my brain. But if I'd been taken from the hospital after birth and dropped into a forest to be raised by wolves—I mean, wolves who hadn't mastered grammar and calculus—I think it's fair to say I wouldn't have won the contest.

Abilities are skills you learn to do.

They may or may not come naturally but you develop them over time.

Writing came naturally, and then I developed my writing skills in English 101 and Creative Writing classes.

Calculus, on the other hand, did not come naturally. But I

liked numbers, I paid attention in class, I did my homework, and I stayed up late the night before most tests doing sample problems.

I had developed my *abilities* in both math and writing.

Let's take a breather from academics for a sec, shall we?

I have a friend named Kelly who is *built* like a runner. Her hips are narrow. Her legs are long. Her thighs and buttocks are muscly. It turns out that she is a naturally gifted athlete.

Kelly has always had the choice of whether she would develop her ability to run or not.

When we were in high school, Kelly might have chosen to walk home after school every day instead of showing up faithfully to track practice. She could have stopped by the gas station convenience store before she got home to buy Cheetos and Mountain Dew. (Yeah, yeah, I know. They sound an awful lot like Reese's and Dr. Pepper. Don't get distracted. Pay attention.) When she got home, Kelly could have fallen into the sofa, ripped open her dusty orange Cheetos, snapped the top off her Mountain Dew, and turned on *Judge Judy*.

Had she made those choices, Kelly still would have been naturally gifted by God with athletics. But Kelly never would have succeeded in the ways that she did—first place in regionals for the 100 hurdles!—if she'd not invested in developing her abilities.

Every day Kelly was one of the first girls to jog to the track, stretch, and start warming up. Whatever our coach asked us to do, Kelly gave 110 percent. She was even that girl who'd get in workouts on the weekends.

Kelly succeeded because she developed her abilities.

Sometimes other people can see our abilities better than we can.

Maybe your grandma likes to tell the story at family gatherings about the time you slept over at her house and how she found you awake reading *Forbes* magazine at two in the morning. (If that weird thing happened, you know your family's never gonna stop talking about it.)

Or perhaps you thought you'd try out for the debate team at your school. And after a few weeks your coach pulled you aside to say that you really had promise, and handed you a brochure for a summer camp that focused on speech and debate.

Maybe a youth group leader saw that you'd checked a book out of the church library on early church history, because you wanted to and not because you had to, and she suggested that you entertain the possibility of attending seminary after college.

Or it could be that your dad took you to the batting cages every Saturday morning because he noticed that you had great hand-eye coordination and he wanted you to have the opportunity to develop your skills.

The people in our lives who recognize our leanings, and who challenge us to develop the abilities we've been given, are God's gifts to us on this journey.

My piano teacher, who was also a musician at our church, offered me opportunities to play the piano at church.

My teacher, Mrs. Gladney, encouraged me to use my academic ability.

Mr. London, on staff at church, encouraged me to sing my first solo in worship.

My boss, at my second job when I was a teen, promoted me for doing excellent work.

As we're keeping our eyes open to notice who God is calling us to become, these people are so important as part of the process. Mine helped me to see several areas that I didn't necessarily think I had a gift for doing, but that I was capable of doing.

⁂

As a child, I took piano lessons until I was fifteen years old. I wish I could tell you I was that kid who rushed home from school every day to practice, but that was not me. It's not that I refused to practice, but let's just say my mom had to remind me. Once or twice.

When I was putting hours into learning notes, forming proper hand and arm posture, and practicing scales and arpeggios, I had no idea that the ability I was developing would be useful to me in any way beyond playing a few Christmas carols for family at the holidays.

In hindsight, though, I can now see that the ability I developed has been an important piece in the combination of gifts, abilities, interests, and nature that make me *Chrystal*.

In my twenties, I led the choir at my church.

Today, as I lay down music tracks for my podcast, in GarageBand, I use the ear that my training developed to choose the melodies with the best rhythm and flow.

I also lead the praise and worship at our church's annual women's conference.

Isn't it cool how that works?

When I was staying up late doing math homework, I had no idea that that ability would open up the possibility of a visit to New York City.

When I was practicing piano I couldn't have imagined GarageBand or how it would help me do what God has called me to do.

In college I was enamored by the sound of so many awesome majors I would have loved to pursue—journalism, English, marketing, psychology, mathematics, Spanish, education, photography, and audio engineering. In the end, I majored in accounting.

Even though it took me a minute to find a job I loved, in my early twenties, I ended up finding my way back to using a lot of the abilities I'd developed over the years. While working for a money management company, I wrote the monthly newsletter. I mean, I was literally writing about money like I had in high school.

If you want to dig deeper to notice what abilities you might have, start thinking about the skills you've learned or are developing.

Maybe you have learned to fold exquisite origami creations. (Don't ask me who will pay you to do this as a job in your twenties. That will be a surprise to us both.)

Or perhaps you volunteered at a veterinarian's office and have been given the opportunity to shadow her and learn a ton about animal care. Maybe she's even taught you how to gently insert a needle under an animal's skin.

If you're like my Kariss, you might have taken the basic sewing skills you learned and continued to study patterns and books to develop your sewing ability.

Or maybe you volunteered at a nonprofit that dismantles and reassembles computers, so you've developed an ability that causes most of us to just scratch our heads.

Having the chance to take cooking classes, play traveling sports, work with a math tutor, or practice your Spanish as a member of Spanish club are all privileges to which not all girls have access. Did you know that girls around the globe can walk up to eight miles, each direction, to fetch water for their families every day? And that long trip that's required for survival often means that these girls don't have the opportunity to attend school. This isn't about giving you a guilt trip. I mention it only to encourage you to value and make the most of the opportunities that you've been afforded.

In what ways, today, can you act like you care about the girl you will be tomorrow? The life you want to live ten or twenty years from now is depending on you to value it right now.

Take the opportunities.
Practice with diligence.
Try new things.
Choose to engage in the business of becoming you.

Reflections for the Rescue

REMEMBER

The abilities you develop offer clues
about who you're made to be.

REFLECT

- What are some of the abilities that you've learned
  so far? Which ones are common to everyone, and
  which are more unique to you?
- Sometimes others recognize our abilities better
  than we can. Have you heard folks in your family
  remark on or tell others about your abilities?
- Are there any opportunities you've been offered,
  or enjoyed, because of your abilities?

RESPOND

After creating a comprehensive list of your abilities,
cross off the ones lots of folks have (cook breakfast,
run a mile)—ask Mom or Dad for help if you need
to!—and notice which ones are more unique.

DEUTERONOMY 8:18; ACTS 11:29; PHILIPPIANS 4:13;
COLOSSIANS 3:23; I PETER 1:13

CHAPTER 14

Calendars, Piggy Banks, and Spelling Bees

Noticing the interests that attract you

When Akiane Kramarik was four years old, she started drawing, often focusing on spiritual or divine subject matter. When she was eight, Akiane spent forty hours painting a picture of the face of Jesus entitled *Prince of Peace*. The painting features the serene countenance of a Middle Eastern man with brown hair, sun-touched highlights, dark eyes, and a dark brown beard. The piece was featured in the best-selling book and film adaptation *Heaven is for Real*. Today, as a young adult, Akiane continues to produce incredible works of art. Akiane's early interest in art was a clue about the woman she was made to be.

Morgan E. Taylor was six years old when she wrote a book called *Daddy's Little Princess*. After seeing countless pop princesses with white skin, Morgan, who is black, started wondering why only white women could be princesses. When she asked her dad, he told her that anyone could be a princess. So Morgan decided to write a book about princesses of all colors, and her dad helped her. Morgan's interest in both human differences and human value was one of her bread crumbs in discovering who she was made to be and what she'd been designed to do.

Bethany Hamilton won her first surfing competition, the Rell Sunn Menehune, when she was just eight years old. If you've heard Bethany's name before, it may be because of the book and movie *Soul Surfer*, detailing her survival of an attack by a fourteen-foot tiger shark. The attacker severed Bethany's left arm just below the shoulder. As crazy and brave and unbelievable as it sounds, Bethany was back on her board a month later. Having appeared on *The Oprah Winfrey Show*, *The Ellen Degeneres Show*, and so many other media outlets, Bethany continues to surf and inspire others. Bethany's passion for surfing is one of the clues that led her to being the woman God designed her to be.

And then there's Sarafina. You'll never read about Sarafina in the newspaper, see her on the *Ellen Show*, or find her on the Amazon bestseller list. But Sarafina's interests are just as important as Akiane's, Morgan's, and Bethany's. When Sarafina was little, her mom and dad often took Sarafina and her siblings camping. They taught her to hike, fish, make campfires, and cook s'mores. When she bought her first Eno hammock in high school, she began camping with her friends. In college, Sarafina earned a degree in environmental sciences. She went on to earn a master's degree in environmental protection. Today, Sarafina is working to protect the earth that God created. Her interest in nature was one of the sticky, gooey, chocolaty, marshmallow-y, graham cracker crumbs that God gave Sarafina as she was noticing who she'd been created to be.

As we've considered what some of those bread crumbs might be in your life, we're noticing the GAIN that's particular to you: Gifts, Abilities, Interests, and Nature. We've considered the gifts (G) you've been given and the abilities (A) you've developed. The next piece of the puzzle to help you GAIN insight into what you're made for—*you see what I did there?*—is to notice your unique interests (I).

Yes, you're interested in Reese's peanut butter cups. I mean, let's be honest, who's not? But that's not what I'm talking about.

I'm asking you to look for the passions and interests that intrigue, delight, and excite you that are *different* than the ones that light your BFF's fire.

Maybe your friend geeks out every year about the opportunity to enter the school science fair, and you can't tell a proton from an electron.

Maybe your sister devours fashion magazines and trolls the hottest fashion blogs, and you struggle to match your left shoe with your right one. (And you're actually pretty fine if they don't match.)

Maybe your cousin spent 417 hours—yeah, she counted them and told you—prepping for the districtwide spelling bee, and you sometimes forget how to spell your middle name.

Or maybe your best friend at summer camp hits the ski slopes every weekend from November to February, and you would just prefer to be inside, by the fire, under a blanket, sipping hot cocoa.

When I was your age, my best friend was turned on by science—biology, chemistry, physics—and I really didn't give a hoot about any of that.

Noticing the interests of others that don't match yours is one way to begin to get at the interests you do value.

I love computers.

No, let me rephrase that.

I love, love, love, love, love, love, love computers. (Better!)

While I hate to even tell you what computers were like back in the dark ages, I'm committed to keeping it real with you. First of all, there was the size. Because you may own a computer that fits in your purse, please know that these bad boys were big. I mean massive. Probably bigger than the microwave in your kitchen. The screen, with no images, had a black background, and the text glowed bright green. (I know, you're probably longing for one of these retro monstrosities right now.) In middle school and high school I loved taking computer classes. I loved learning everything about them. When I got to college, the classes just had fancier names, like Business Information Systems. (Yeah, you're not fooling me, course catalog. I know we're talking about computers!) I chose to take those classes as electives because I *enjoyed* them.

Becoming proficient in computers as they've evolved over the last few decades is a skill I've continued to develop over the years, but the interest has always been there. And everything I've learned helps me do what I do today as a professional communicator—editing my podcast, posting on my blog, and improving my website. And while I do have help to manage all of that now, I like to keep my fingers in it because I'm interested!

Having a gift or an ability to do something doesn't necessarily mean you enjoy it.

Your interests are what you *enjoy*.

What do you like to do? What do you gravitate toward when you have the space and time to do what makes your soul smile?

Let me ask you a few questions to help you notice the interests you're most passionate about. And, just for the fun of it, let's take "screens" and social off the table.

What do you prefer to do with your time? When you're given a free Saturday, with no responsibilities how do you choose to spend it? And whom do you spend it with?

What about travel? If cost and distance were not obstacles, where would you go? Would you stroll through the Louvre? Attend a rodeo? Snorkel in the Bahamas? Participate in an archaeological dig in the Middle East? Backpack through Germany?

What about education? If you could study anything in college, what would you choose?

What about work? Imagine your dream life a dozen years from now. And really dream big. What are you doing in your job? What do you love most about it?

What about hobbies? Which ones do you most enjoy today? If you had the opportunity, what hobbies would you like to try or develop?

One of the ways we know what we value is to notice how we spend our time, our money, our energy, or our thoughts. These might tip you off to some of your interests too.

When you look at your calendar, what do you see? Yeah, a lot of blocks filled up with what you have to do, but what do you see when you scan the entries of things you *want* to do? Maybe you volunteer at the local animal shelter. Maybe you deliver Meals on Wheels with your dad. Maybe you take thirty-mile bike rides on the weekends. Maybe you sit on the couch and knit awesome gifts for others. Notice how you use your time.

When you look at your bank statements—or, peek inside that ceramic piggy bank your grandma gave you—what do you notice? Are there clues in the way you spend your money that signal what your interests are? Maybe you're the generous friend who treats others to burgers and fries. Or maybe you're the person who invests in a really good telescope, laptop, or car speakers. Or maybe you're a saver. Even that is a clue! (Hey, what are you saving for? Tell me . . .)

How are you spending your energy and thoughts? Do you get fired up about injustice? Do you think constantly about ways that your school cafeteria could be so much better than it is? Are you passionate about the plight of endangered animals? Do you keep a sketchbook with inventions you'll create and market one day? Notice what fills your mind and uses your energy. Those signal your interests.

Your passions, your interests, set your soul on fire. They light you up. They get you excited. They're the things you can't stop talking about—and don't want to stop talking about. Those passions and interests are *God-given*. When God made you, He was intentional in uniquely crafting you. Your interests are part of who you are, and it's important to pay attention to them.

You never know how God will use those interests in the future.

Reflections for the Rescue

REMEMBER

Your interests offer clues to who God made you to be.

REFLECT

- Is there something you enjoy so much that you think about it when you're not doing it?
- Are there activities you've enjoyed since you were a child, and still like to do?
- Your interests are what you want to do when you have a choice. When will you make time to read His love letter to you and listen for His direction?

RESPOND

As you think about your interests and all you enjoy, which ones make you smile? Scroll through your mental list and notice which ones bring you that joy.

---

1 CORINTHIANS 10:31, ACTS 6:1–4, ECCLESIASTES 9:10, 1 SAMUEL 10:7, NEHEMIAH 2, ACTS 17:28

CHAPTER 15

Extroverts, Introverts, and Everyone in Between

Noticing your nature

If you met my friend Madeline, it might take you a bit to figure her out.

Some people think she's an extrovert because she's really comfortable speaking in front of audiences. She's animated in conversations. She's not a bit shy.

Once you get to know Madeline, you discover that she's an introvert. Being at parties, mingling at church, and even pushing her way through the Saturday morning farmer's market saps her energy. To recharge, Madeline needs to spend time walking in nature, reading, or writing on her laptop.

Madeline is a very confident and competent person, so a lot people are surprised when they find out that she's among the fifteen to twenty percent of the population who might be labeled as Highly Sensitive Persons, or HSP.

If Madeline walks into a restaurant and discovers loud music and a dozen tables of people trying to talk over the sound, she feels so overwhelmed by the stimulation that she'll turn around and walk out. If the television is on at home and someone speaks to Madeline, she's not able to process either sound. Even driving in a car on the way to an awesome beach vacation, Madeline's senses are keenly aware of the CD that's playing, two kids talking in the backseat, alerts on her teenagers' phones, the sound and feel of the air-conditioning blowing on her, and the roar of eighteen-wheelers passing by. Should the phone ring on that trip, Madeline is already too overwhelmed to answer it.

Madeline is a writer, by profession, so people also assume she must be a big reader. Although Madeline doesn't advertise it, nothing could be further from the truth. When she's tried to read fiction, she often struggles to follow the narrative, having to reread passages several times. She does a little better reading *People* magazine, LOL, because blocks of words are much shorter. When she joins her community for prayer, she no longer tries to follow along in the prayer book, which requires turning ahead several pages at a time. She will either pray silently or look on at a neighbor's prayer book. Even when Madeline goes to a restaurant, she typically orders one of the first two items off the menu, because she has trouble wading through so many words. (Totally crazy that she's a writer, right?)

Madeline sometimes feels ashamed of the unique way that she seems to have been hardwired because our culture places a high value on extroverts, multi-tasking, and competencies like reading. And I know Madeline has been tempted to squeeze herself into a different-shaped mold, trying to be someone she's not. She'll show up at parties she knows will wear her out because she thinks she should. She might not let on in conversation that she hasn't read the hottest new book everyone is talking about. Or she'll *hold* a prayer book—funny, right?—to give the appearance that she's doing what everyone expects her to do.

I get exhausted just thinking about it.

Of course, we all have versions of playing the same game, don't we?

If we're naturally shy or more reserved, we'll make a huge effort to mingle at the school football game.

If we're not athletically inclined, we might go out on a limb to roller skate if we're invited to a 70s-themed roller disco party.

If we're hyper-organized, we might find ourselves taking deep calming breaths in the chaotic vacation cabin that a dozen messy family members are sharing.

If we can't dance, we don't want to look like a total wallflower, so we'll talk to people we don't even know, or worse, attempt to go out on the dance floor and just sway a bit without really showing that we can't dance *for real.*

If we make decisions based on our emotions, we might work really hard to create a list of pros and cons for each college we're considering.

We do it because it's socially appropriate.
We do it because we're in a situation over which we
    have no control.
We do it out of our love for someone else.

We do it because it's wise.

Sure, at times we all need to flex a bit when it comes to operating outside of the way we're naturally wired. Sometimes, all of us need to behave in ways that take us outside of our comfort zones.

But as we continue to think about what it means to show up for your life, I'm encouraging you to take a closer look at the way you're wired. What type of nature has been knit into the very fiber of who you are.

A friend of mine worked as a physical therapist in a residential facility for people with disabilities. Every resident had an annual meeting to discuss his or her progress medically, socially, intellectually, etc. Nurses, teachers, and speech/physical/occupational therapists attended these meetings. One day Janie attended a meeting for a resident named Denise, who was about to be added to Janie's PT roster. Because Janie hadn't spent much time with Denise, she only knew what she'd witnessed of Denise when she'd seen her in her bedroom, the hallway, or one of the building's classrooms. Often Denise would be raising her voice with loud insistent shouts. Other times she'd be banging a coffee cup on the wooden door of her room. With her limited human vision, it was hard for Janie to identify what was special, precious, and unique about Denise.

When Denise's teacher offered her report, Janie finally understood.

With a knowing grin on her face, Denise's teacher said, "Denise is an advocate. She knows what she wants, and she makes sure that other people know too. And she *loves* her some coffee! We have lots of residents who might like a cup of coffee but would be too shy to ask for it. Not Denise! When she wants coffee, we know about it."

Janie's eyes were opened to one of the many ways that Denise was uniquely hardwired. And once she was aware of it, she was better able to befriend Denise and help her to become all that she had been created to be.

Our nature describes our natural personalities (when we're not hurt or hungry or tired).

Some people are naturally extroverted.
Others are naturally introverted.
Some people love to pick a fight, just for the fun of it.
Others are peacemakers.
Some folks walk into a room and light it up with their natural charisma.
Others prefer to slip in unnoticed and observe those around them.
Some folks are passionate about advocating for social justice.
Others prefer to be a caregiver, meeting the needs of one person.

Those last two lines are great examples of why we need all types of people to show up for their lives. The world needs those who will organize and speak up for justice for many. And the world also needs those who will focus their attention on meeting the physical, social, emotional, or intellectual needs of just one person.

And that's exactly why it's so important that you embrace and celebrate and honor your unique nature. When you embrace who you really are, you free up others to embrace and live into who they really are.

So where are you most likely to feel like you're being the best *you* that you can be?

Is it organizing a walkout at your school to stand in solidarity with students who suffered an attack at their school?

Or is it raising money to provide mental health services for survivors?

Are you the girl who's going to be the first one to show up at a party, talk to every single person there, and be the last one to leave?

Or are you going to show up, check it out, and then ditch it with your best friend to go to an all-night pancake restaurant?

Are you the girl in the front row of the concert with raised hands, banging your head?

Or are you happier chillin' in the back row, taking it all in?

Your wiring is beautiful.

Let me say that again.

Your personality is a part of your unique and wonderful design. While we all have the opportunity to become the

Don't *mistake* being the best version of yourself for being like *someone else*.

best versions of ourselves, don't mistake being the best version of yourself for being like someone else.

Honoring your personality is an important part of showing up for your life. Because if you don't do it, who will?

A number of years ago, when I was feeling stuck and unhappy in my job, I decided to take a long hard look at my gifts, abilities, interests, and nature. One afternoon, I made a cup of hot tea, then sat with pen in hand and thought about what in me might still be valuable, useful, and notable.

On a blank sheet of paper, I wrote the words "strengths," "weaknesses," "passions," and "personality traits." (You can hear how those are pretty much: **g**ifts, **a**bilities, **i**nterests, and **n**ature, right?) I underlined each word and sat pensively, staring at the page while waiting for my thoughts to flow. And let me tell ya, I sat there for a while. The thoughts came but they didn't *flow fast*. It was more like a drip from a leaky bathroom faucet.

I was a little disillusioned with how my life had gone so far, but I decided to take inventory so I could figure out where to go next. I thought that I'd headed in the wrong direction in my career because I hadn't carefully identified the cargo I was carrying and aligned that knowledge with an appropriate destination.

Honestly, it wasn't just about the job.

I wanted to put down on paper the parts of me I'd forgotten about, walked away from, dismissed, or devalued because of drifts, decisions, and collisions.

I struggled at first to write much. I didn't realize how much my self-destructive thoughts, habits, and actions had affected me. I had a hard time finding "the gift of me" underneath the rubble of my circumstances and the debris of painful experiences.

But I sat. I looked. I listened.

After awhile, a few words came. They didn't come fast, but they came.

I kept listening. And I persisted in writing down the thoughts that came to mind. While I didn't get much on paper that first day, I kept the piece of paper near and pulled it out here and there. I slowly realized how important it was to pay attention to the unique material God had given me to work with and to think about my life. The more I took the time to notice, the more I noticed what was there.

Over time, the list grew, one word at a time, until I'd uncovered more of what God had given me that I'd buried.

If you're inclined to writing, like I am, start a Word doc and begin to chronicle all that you and others have noticed that make you *you*.

If that's not your jam, create a note on your phone. Add to it when you notice sparks of joy, satisfaction, and delight inside you.

Knowing who God has designed you to be, and noticing the qualities and skills you've developed along the way, is going to equip you to *show up well* for the unique life that is yours.

Reflections for the Rescue

REMEMBER

Your nature, or your natural hardwiring,
gives you clues about who you are.

REFLECT

- The way you are wired matters. What do you notice about your natural way of being in the world? How is it like others, and how is it unlike others?
- There's no wrong way to be wired. Are there natural characteristics in you that others don't value? How do you use them for good?
- The world needs you to be who you really are. Trying to fit into someone else's mold is exhausting. How will you commit to honoring your unique nature?

RESPOND

Create two columns, listing your natural tendencies in the left-hand column. Then, on the right, brainstorm ways that your unique nature can benefit God's world.

PSALM 119, GENESIS 1:27, JOSHUA 1, JUDGES 7

CHAPTER 16

Be a Moving Target

you don't have to know it all

You may know Letitia Wright from her role in a little movie called *The Black Panther*. She plays Shuri, the spicy sister of T'Challa, King of Wakanda. Her character is dynamic, smart, and funny, and Wright's performance is a delight.

What you may not know is that Letitia, who'd pursued acting for years, eventually decided to take a break from the craft to pursue a relationship with God. While those two things aren't mutually exclusive, she obeyed when she felt the nudge to pause her acting pursuits. Wright had devoted herself to acting but still felt a void in her heart. So she made space for a season to focus on her soul. She'd been looking for value in one thing and had neglected to pay attention to the *whole* thing.

As is so often the case when we're obedient to God, Letitia was finally filled with a security that didn't depend on scoring a particular role, starring alongside A-list actors, or

151

winning shiny gold trophies. During the season she devoted to the Lord, her happiness and satisfaction became dependent only on her relationship with God.

So it's a bit ironic that she was offered the role of Shuri after she'd stopped chasing the thing she'd so desperately wanted. Rather than continuing to bang her head against a wall, traipsing from audition to audition, Letitia was faithful to do what was right in front of her, which was tending to the hole in her heart.

She went with what she knew and God took care of the rest.

When Letitia said yes to God, she couldn't have foreseen the avalanche of blessings that were coming her way.

And I want you to hear that you don't have to see the whole picture.

You don't have to predict, today, what's coming down the road for you.

You don't even have to know what your college major will be.

God is asking you only to be faithful to what you *do* know.

To do what's right in front of you.

⁓

A common problem many of us will face in our lifetime is that we want to know *the* answer for how best to live fully and know we've given our best shot at our one opportunity to walk this earth.

For some of us, *the* answer seems to elude us.

And looking for *the* answer stresses us out.

We tend to glorify people who seem to have it all figured out.

The class valedictorian who will continue his groundbreaking cancer research when he attends Harvard on a full-ride scholarship.

That girl who started drawing when she was four and now sells paintings for thousands of dollars.

The classmate who's been training to be an Olympic gymnast since she was two.

The boy who raised $15,000 so that a village in Africa could have access to clean running water.

Those are some strong college application essays right there; am I right?

These kids appear to know exactly where they're headed and how they'll go about getting there. As for the rest of us, well, not knowing *the* answer might make us feel a little challenged, like something is wrong or maybe we were sleeping when God was handing out passion and purpose. I've often felt like the "dunce" in the back of the class who missed e-v-e-r-y-t-h-i-n-g.

It can be frustrating to want to honor your girl by living a life she will be proud of but not know exactly how to make that happen.

Part of loving your life is learning to be *content* and *appreciating* each step you take.

Well, let me take some of the pressure off you.

Your job is not to find *the* answer that leads to a master-plan or purpose. Your job is to move forward as you become aware of *an* answer you can act on. You must accept that *an* answer is part of the process to getting to *the* answer.

Part of loving your life is learning to be content, appreciating each step you take, and believing that even *an* answer is good enough for right now.

Your answer for today can lead you to *the* answer for tomorrow.

That's what happened for Letitia Wright. When she honored God with her choices, unexpected doors of opportunity opened up for her.

Remember how we talked about your unique design and your unique experiences? When you are looking for *an* answer, simply start by looking at what's already inside you and what experiences and opportunities you already have access to. Be a good steward of those gifts.

Build on the gifts God gave you. Don't minimize them or mistakenly *perceive* them as small.

Build on the gifts God gave you. Don't minimize them or mistakenly perceive them as small or insignificant. This is an error many of us make and make often. We diminish the gifts we've been endowed with, then wonder why *the* answers do not rise up to greet us. God has already given you the raw material you need to build a life worth living. There is your answer.

While I've shared with you how I noticed the bread crumbs God put in my path, what I didn't tell you was that I've spent a lot of time being a whiny brat when the bread crumbs didn't seem to present themselves fast enough or take me where I thought I wanted to go.

I didn't understand that the seemingly insignificant answers were part of my progress. However, over time I've gained new perspective. When we act on *an* answer, using what God has given us and using it well, we honor our process and give God something to work with.

I've heard my father say a million times, "God loves to hit a moving target." It's true. God is best able to work with those who are already in motion! We are more apt to find *the* answer when we're willing to move on with what we can know and do today. And how exactly do you move forward? You practice who you are and what you love. By moving on with the answers available to you, you will also be moving toward more answers waiting to be discovered.

Practice who you are and what you love.

Misty Copeland, the first African-American female principal dancer with the American Ballet Theatre, didn't grow up dreaming about being a professional ballerina. She grew up in a single-parent home where there wasn't really extra money for dance lessons. But Misty did know she loved to dance, so she joined the drill team at her school.

The team coach noticed her natural ability and recommended she take ballet at the local Boys and Girls Club. Misty's gift continued to open doors for her as she discovered a growing passion for a direction in her life she didn't even know was possible.[5]

Recognize what God has put in you. Notice what brings you joy and satisfies your soul. Acknowledge your experiences, recognize your pain, and see all that God has allowed into your life as the stuff that can fill your soul, but not define it. Then move toward some answer—and trust that doing so engages you with the girl only you can be.

I'm virtually positive that Celine Dion loves doing what she does for a living. Oprah probably does too. I grew up watching Janet Jackson dancing on stage, moving her hips in ways I couldn't fathom doing with my own. She loves dancing, and it shows. Who wouldn't want to spend their lives doing something they love, something that seems to be *the* answer for their lives?

Many of us spend a lot of time looking at people who have widely recognized gifts, talents, or experiences, and we wish we had the answers they've been able to find. Some people that we know—or think we know because of Instagram—seem to have it so together. Things always seem to go their way. Even the lighting in their photos. We see their product but don't value their process. If we did, we'd more highly value our own. If we valued what we love, we would celebrate, work at, cultivate, and appreciate those gifts. If we value our gifts,

we might realize we're just as much in love with our lives as we imagine others to be in love with theirs, even if our hips won't move in the ways we wish them to.

Celebrities aren't the only ones who find the answers. *Anyone* who is faithful to their progress can live fully. I have the confidence, and you can have the confidence, that "he who began a good work in you will carry it on to completion until the day of Christ Jesus" (Philippians 1:6).

We all do it the same way—*an* answer at a time.

Reflections for the Rescue

REMEMBER

Build on the gifts God gave you.

REFLECT

- What can you do to build on the gifts God has given you?
- Are you making room to do things that you love? Why or why not?
- What is *an* answer you can take action on today?

RESPOND

Since you are the steward of the gifts, abilities, interests, and nature God has given you, what small step can you take today to build on what you've been given? Consider what you can do to develop the gift of you.

PHILIPPIANS 3:13–14; MATTHEW 25:14–30;
MARK 12:41–44; LUKE 16:10; PSALM 90:12

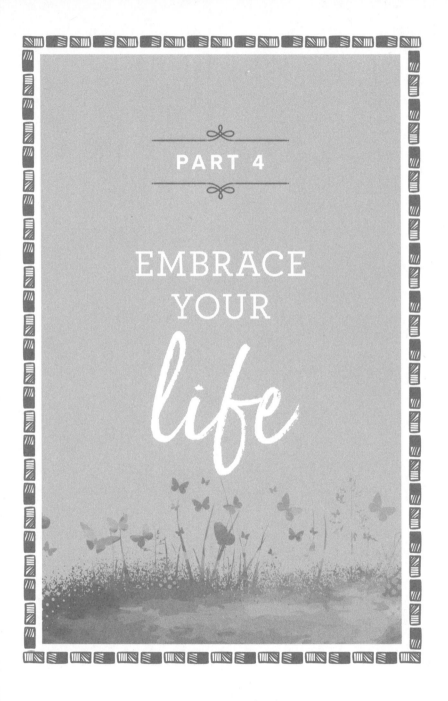

PART 4

EMBRACE
YOUR
life

Wiggling My Toes in My Fuzzy Rug

Nurturing your soul

When I was fifteen, I had the opportunity to travel with my youth group on a mission trip to Guatemala.

Y'all, just the bus ride from the airport in Guatemala City to our host village, through the lush mountainous region, was life-changing. Did I fear I was going to *lose* my life if the van plummeted over the side of the steep winding embankments? I absolutely did. But between terror-filled moments of squeezing my eyes shut, I drank in the majestic beauty of this gorgeous country. The tree-lined mountains were breathtaking.

The further we got from the city, the more peaceful and happy I felt. Without the distractions of my regular teenage life, I remember thinking, "I feel so *alive*."

As we neared the village where we'd be spending a week, we crossed over a narrow one-lane bridge. Peering out the dusty windows of the bus, I could see women bent over, washing clothes in the river.

Throughout the week, all the new sights, sounds, and smells filled me in a way that's hard to express. Maybe the best way to say it is that the experience filled my tank.

To this day, I experience a similar feeling of fullness and satisfaction when I have the opportunity to sit in a park, surrounded by towering trees. Honestly, I even love looking out my kitchen window at the trees in our yard.

Right now my family is looking for a new home, and I've been really clear with my husband: It has to be on a treed lot.

Now, I have friends who live in the city, at the beach, or even in the desert. I can see that they are completely content where they are. That's how I've learned that what makes me feel happy, settled, and peaceful might be different for someone else. In a way, noticing what fills us up is similar to noticing our gifts, abilities, interests, and nature. Because each one of us is uniquely designed, like no other in the whole world, what fills us up will be unique as well.

Some women I know recharge their batteries by going to the gym. (Bless their hearts.)

Others refuel by picking out a good book and curling up on the couch to read for hours.

One woman I know is re-energized by walking to the tunes of '70s soul, funk, and rhythm and blues. (I see you, Margot.)

Another woman is refreshed and replenished by a swim in the ocean.

Okay, well, maybe you don't have access to your own

private ocean. Let's go with that. The things that fill your tank and nurture your soul, don't have to be quite that grand.

> Maybe it's stroking your cat as he sits peacefully in your lap. Until he doesn't.
> Maybe it's making and drinking an icy cold fruit smoothie.
> Maybe it's lying face down on your hot sun-soaked driveway on a cool day.
> Maybe it's dipping your hands in finger paints and creating a masterpiece.

When I was a kid, my mom decorated our bedrooms. As moms do. The first bedroom that my sister and I shared was Strawberry Shortcake themed. If you don't know Strawberry Shortcake, you might be picturing a dessert-themed room, which, I have to admit, would be awesome. But Strawberry Shortcake was actually an animated character in the '80s and '90s who looked a little bit like a rag doll but has since been updated. She wears a strawberry hat, a smocked shirt, striped leggings, and pink shoes. And she has a little friend who's a cat. Now you know.

When I got too old for Strawberry, my mom redecorated our room, with custom-made bedding, in navy and mauve. I'm not gonna lie; I didn't like it. I was a big girl and I wanted something that expressed that. I wanted something jazzier than what navy and mauve could provide.

So when I was getting ready to leave for college, I dreamed of decorating my dorm room. Specifically, I wanted something that screamed, "I'm here!" When my mom and I went shopping, I chose a bed-in-a-bag from Wal-Mart, containing all the bedding I needed for my room, including a white bedspread with splashes of bright yellow, neon blue, black, and pink. (Gotta love the '90s.) I also begged my mom to buy this white high-pile plush rug. When my mom warned me that it would get quickly dirty, I continued to plead. Friend, can I just tell you how happy it made me to walk around that little dorm room barefoot? I loved the feel of the fuzzy shag pile under my feet. It just made something inside me go *ooooohhhhh*. (Oh yeah, my mom was totally right about the dirt. Respect, Mom.)

Of course there are lots of other ways I nurture my soul. I'm totally that girl who digs curling up with a good book.

I've always known that God loves me but looking back I realize that I often forgot He also gives me permission to love myself, embrace my life, and delight in simple joys.

Trees.
Fuzzy rugs.
Bright colors.
Chocolate that melts in my mouth.

God didn't just create me; He created this wonderful world in which I live, and He intends for me to engage wholeheartedly with it, not neglecting to take care of my soul, which is the most important part of who I am.

Whether you are hustling to take four Advanced Placement classes, work a part-time job, volunteer on weekends, stay active in your church, or help care for a younger sibling, you still get to participate with God in caring for the real you.

So what are the things that light your fire?

Seeing a rainbow?
Eating banana pudding?
Soaking in a hot tub?
Running in the rain?

The things that nurture your soul don't have to make sense to anyone else besides you. But they will restore you by making you feel a little lighter, a little more settled, a little more peaceful.

How do you go about filling up your soul?

You were created with five senses—sight, smell, touch, taste, and hearing. Your physical body is a God-given way to perceive and experience your world.

You fill your soul when your eyes take in the words on the pages of a favorite book. You feast deeply on inspiration when you watch athletes at the top of their game, hear music that inspires, or touch the soft fur of a puppy.

I mean, doesn't something change in you immediately when you walk into Bath and Body Works and smell "spa"?

When is the last time you engaged your God-given senses and something caused you to smile, close your eyes with pleasure, or breathe deeply, taking it all in?

If you can't remember, it's probably been too long.

The simple joy of significant relationships will spark a

wonderful sense of satisfaction in your soul. It's natural to want to know that we're significant in the estimation of other human beings. That we are seen and that we matter. That someone cares whether we are here, and that another person is a witness to our life.

We were designed with connection in mind. God Himself exists in constant connection. He knows community—Father, Son, and Holy Spirit—and designed us in His image, so it's no wonder we desire the same. We were created with a soul that needs to feel significant, and we need to share that significance with others. Yes, God uses the people in our lives to reflect our value and worth.

Significance is a gift to be received.

Making time for 5:00 a.m. cups of coffee with my friends has been a remedy for me during seasons when my days seem full. I have learned to communicate with those who care about me when I need their ear, their time, or both of their arms to squeeze me hard when the days are tough.

I've learned it's okay to have a healthy need for people who love, affirm, and care genuinely for the girl in me.

Relationships fill our cup—relationships with people who know us, value us, and treasure us.

And they should.

One important note: your sense of significance can never *depend* on the attention of others. Parents get overwhelmed. Friends get flaky. And boys—who may *never* realize that you are the most amazing girl at your school, in your state, and on this planet—can be clueless. Can I get an *amen*?

Now, before I sound like a free-spirited flower child who is out of touch with reality, let me assure you that I know what you're thinking.

Honey, I'm in a jacked-up place in my life, and you think a fuzzy rug is going to help?!

Well, yes, I do!

If that's what does it for ya.

I also want to tell you that the joy that can fill your soul through your senses and significance is temporary.

That kind of joy doesn't last.

It can't.

We live in an imperfect world with rainy days and acne and missing homework assignments.

We also live in a world where people aren't perfect. So your sense of significance and joy can never *depend* on the attention of others. Graciously, there is One whose attention to us and love for us does not fail.

That's why your knowledge of who you are is so important. You are a soul in a body designed to be filled by the Spirit.

It's simple. Know God, love Him, and seek to please Him, and you will know an unexplainable joy that simply overflows. If that sounds like a burdensome task list, listen again: When you offer yourself to God, God will fill you with joy and delight.

Choose to nurture your soul by cultivating joy.

Nurturing your soul is about paying attention to the people, places, things, and experiences that make you feel alive.

That fill you with a sense of peace.

That bring you joy.

Slowing down, paying attention, and appreciating the beauty around you is a choice.

So I choose.

I choose to ride the amusement park rollercoasters with my family in the dead heat of summer.

I choose to wake up every morning and stream music from one of my playlists that will set the tone for my day.

I choose to drink straight out of the milk container now and again for the sheer joy of doing it—and hope that no one else in the house catches me.

I choose to spend time with those I love, looking them in the eye instead of staring at the device in my hand.

I choose to look for ways to give to others who can't return the favor, knowing that my gift to them is also a gift to me.

I choose to make time for the study of His Word, to get to know Him better, and to learn His principles for a well-lived life.

I believe that you can choose too.

Even if it means choosing a fuzzy rug that is going to attract dirt.

Reflections for the Rescue

REMEMBER

Choose to nurture your soul by cultivating joy.

REFLECT

- Simple joys matter. What can you engage in with your sight, smell, touch, taste, and hearing that will make you smile?
- Significant relationships matter. What person should you make time to talk to or be with? Give them a call or send them a text and plan a time to hang out.
- The Spirit of God gives joy. When will you make time to read His love letter to you and listen for His direction?

RESPOND

Make a list of things that nurture your soul and give you energy. Post the list in plain view. Refer to it often.

ZEPHANIAH 3:17; PSALM 16:11; JEREMIAH 31:13;
ECCLESIASTES 9:7; ROMANS 15:13; NEHEMIAH 8:9–10;
PROVERBS 17:22; PHILIPPIANS 4:4; PSALM 30:5

CHAPTER 18

Malala, Joni, and You

Do what you can with what you have

When I was in high school, I was a proud member of Duncanville High School's flag corps. Go Panthers!

If your school doesn't have flag corps, imagine about thirty girls wearing blue and white rhinestone-studded costumes, running alongside the band during halftime at the big Friday night football game, and waving huge flags. After being on the corps for two years, I got it in my mind that I wanted to try out to be captain of the team.

You know I would have killed it, right? I was enthusiastic. Organized. Not afraid to boss people around when the situation called for it. I thought I'd make a great captain.

There was just one little snafu interfering with me achieving my dream.

The team always started practicing at the end of July so that we'd be ready for the team's first football game at the beginning of September. But my family always went on vacation together for two weeks in August, and my dad's rule was that none of us could miss family vacation. I knew I couldn't be captain if I was going to miss two weeks of practice in August.

"PUH-LEASE, DAD?!?!" I begged, one night after dinner. "I really, really, really, really wanna try out for captain!"

Nothing about my dad's expression suggested that he was moved . . . at all . . . by my pleading. And, having lived with him for sixteen years, I knew that there was no way he'd allow me to miss vacation. I just had to do all of the begging so that he knew how much I'd be missing because of his dumb rule.

I went on vacation.

I wasn't named captain.

At the time, it felt like my world was ending.

However, I did get co-captain.

And then something my aunt once said to me bubbled up in my heart. It's still a principle I try to live by today: Do what you can with what you have.

So I decided to give 100 percent to flag corps. And you know what? I got to participate in something I really enjoyed. I was privileged to be in a leadership role. And I made great memories with my friends. I did what I could with what I had. I'd always known from reading my Bible that contentment is important. So in this season, I chose to follow my aunt's advice and live like I believed it regardless of whether I thought I had much to live it with.

> Don't wait until you're president of the student body
> before trying to make a difference at your school.

Don't wait to start saving money for college until your
senior year.

Don't wait to get involved in extracurricular activities
until you're starting to fill out college applications.

Don't wait to have a party until you finally wedge your
way into a circle of cooler girls.

Do what you can to live your life well with what
you have.

It's tempting to get
hung up on what we want
to do. We can even get bent
out of shape when it doesn't
happen. But our plans are
not always the same as
God's plans.

Do what you can with
what you have.

> Do what you
> can to *live* your
> life *well* with
> what you have.

❧

In the region of Pakistan where Malala Yousafzai was born
and raised, the local Taliban had, at various times, banned
girls from attending school. After a documentary featured
Malala speaking out about the right to learn, people began
to recognize her, locally and internationally, for her thoughts
and activism. When she was fifteen, Malala and two other
girls were shot while riding a bus home from school. The
attack was in retaliation for Malala's activism. Fortunately,
Malala survived, going on to co-author the best-selling *I Am*

Malala, as well as receive the 2014 Nobel Peace Prize at the age of seventeen.

Malala Yousafzai didn't wake up one day and decide to become the most famous teenager in the world. No, little by little, day by day, she did what she could with what she had. When she was eleven, she had a keyboard and a blog. After she was featured in Adam B. Ellick's documentary, several news outlets interviewed her. She responded to the opportunities that came her way.

That's what I'm inviting you to do.

It starts with doing what you can with what you have to work with today and trusting that over time it will make a difference.

You just never know what can come tomorrow from doing what you can do today.

> You just never know what can come *tomorrow* from doing what you can do *today*.

Sometimes it's as simple as embracing what brings you joy and fills your soul.

I've always wondered how Mother Teresa became Mother Teresa—a woman renowned worldwide for taking care of others.

After all the accolades and attention, the bottom line is that Mother Teresa loved people. She knew that serving the needy filled her soul, and she faithfully allowed her life to overflow to others. She didn't start with fame or notoriety. She didn't wait until she had just the right set of circumstances, the ideal amount of money, or a certain number of people paying attention. She simply honored the love in her heart and the call on her life and embraced the opportunities she had.

Sometimes doing what you can also involves pushing through pain.

Almost fifty years ago, Joni Eareckson Tada became a paraplegic after diving into a lake and severing her spinal cord. She has not had use of her legs or arms since she was a teenager. During the darkest times of her life and seasons of great physical and emotional pain, she decided to rediscover her love of art and figure out how to once again participate in creative work. Joni learned how to paint by holding a paintbrush with her mouth. Her artwork began selling, and this inspired her to do more with her life.

Many people know about Joni because, ten years after her accident, she wrote her own autobiography of her difficult journey. A few years later, that story became a movie. For many years, Joni has championed the cause of those with physical disabilities and told people about her love for God.

But ultimately, Joni really focused on doing what she could with what she had. She had a creative spirit. She had a mouth. She had a paintbrush.

Maya Angelou had a painful past and a pen. She did what she could with what she had and is now remembered as a brilliant poet. She gave words to thousands of people who make sense of their experiences through her writings.

Doing the best you can with what you have has a funny

way of giving birth to surprising new paths and perspectives. In fact, God proves over and over in the Scriptures that He loves to use people who are willing to do what they can with what they have.

God *proves* over and over in the Scriptures that He loves to use people who are *willing* to do what they can with what they have.

When Moses questioned God's call on his life, God asked Moses to use what he had—a common stick used to guide sheep—to deliver half a million people out of Israel (Exod. 4:1–5).

When, as a young man, David experienced a burning passion to defend God's glory, God enabled him to do what a whole army was unwilling to do. David faced a giant and knocked him out with what he had—a pebble and a slingshot (1 Sam. 17:22–40).

When Jesus and His disciples were discussing solutions for feeding five thousand hungry people, a little boy allowed the disciples to have his five fish and two loaves of bread. He was willing to make his next meal available for God's use and believed that Jesus could do something with what little he had to give (John 6:8–10).

God not only invites you to do what you can with what

you have, but He also requires you to do so. For you to experience the fullness of what He can do in and through your life, He calls you to engage in your life.

Let me say this as plainly as I can. You. Have. To. LIVE. Not as a passive bystander of life. Move through each day as purposefully and intentionally as you can. Your life is not a dress rehearsal. Each day that passes is a day you will never see again.

In Matthew 25:14–30, Jesus tells the story of a man who entrusted different levels of wealth in the form of talents to three of his servants before he planned to be absent for a time. Upon his return, the man asked for an account of those assets. He expected that while he was away, the servants would use what they had to return more to him than they'd received.

The servant who had received five talents doubled his investment and now had ten. The servant who had been given two talents doubled his investment and now had four. But the man who'd been given one talent did nothing with what he had. Afraid he would bumble the job, he simply sat around and waited. And his master showed no sympathy for the servant's reasoning to play it safe and hope for the best. Instead, he chided him for his failure to try.

You may feel overwhelmed by what you don't know. I get it. I don't like that feeling either. But don't be overwhelmed. Don't get bogged down by what you can or can't do right now. You don't have to have the perfect perspective, feel completely satisfied in your soul, or be totally past your pain.

You only need to be faithful to do what you can with what you have and what you know right now.

Maybe you can't afford canvas or an art class, but what if you use your pencil to draw regularly in your sketchbook?

Maybe your family can't afford the four-year degree right now, but how about starting your higher education at the local community college or online?

You might not have a huge group of friends, but what about being the very best friend you can be to the girls who are your friends? And maybe a few more who'd like to be your friend?

Choose every day to wake up and find one thing you can do to honor the beautiful being you are and the beautiful life only you can live. Before you know it, you'll see the girl in you coming out of the shadows.

Reflections for the Rescue

REMEMBER

You never know what can come tomorrow
from doing what you can do today.

REFLECT

- What has God given you to work with?
- Do you feel like God can use you? Why or why not?
- What actions or opportunities are in front of you? Are you acting on them? Why or why not?

RESPOND

Don't focus on what you can't do. Think about what is possible. What does "doing what you can" look like right now? Make a list of actions you can take right now, big or small. Remember, you can always do *something*.

EXODUS 3:1–14; 4:1–17; JUDGES 7:2–8; 1 PETER 4:10–11;
1 TIMOTHY 4:14; LUKE 16:11; MATTHEW 25:14–30;
COLOSSIANS 3:23–25; PROVERBS 18:16; COLOSSIANS 3:17

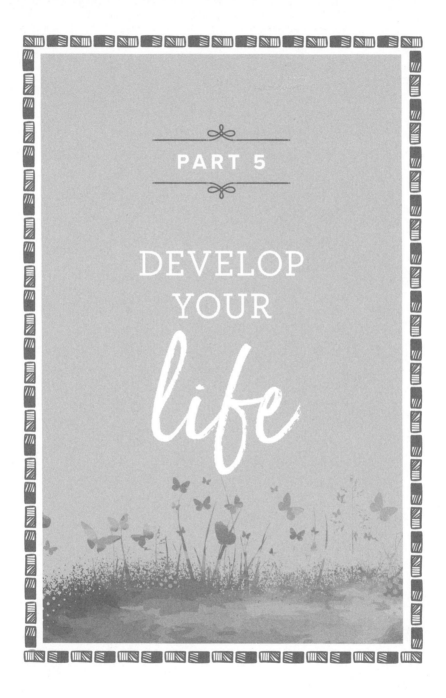

PART 5

DEVELOP
YOUR
life

CHAPTER 19

Eyes on the Prize

Focus on the finish

On my high school track team, I really wanted to be a super-fast sprinter. I wanted to run a blazingly fast 100 and fly past every other competitor in the 200.

Alas, that was not to be my role.

The event my coach chose for me, that required longer endurance more than a shorter burst of speed, was the 800. Eight hundred meters is two laps around the track. It's far, but it's not far *enough* to be able to get away with jogging or walking. No, it still pretty much requires an all-out effort. But instead of sprinting for 100 or 200 meters, it's sprinting for 800.

So basically it's brutal.

At a Wednesday afternoon meet, I was slated for the 800.

At the sound of the gun, I burst from the starting line and hit the first 400 pretty hard. But by the time I ran one lap around the track, I began to panic as I realized I had an entire second lap to run.

I could hear my dad screaming my name from the stands. "Go, Chrystal!!!"

His voice faded into the distance as I began the second lap. By that point, my feet were moving forward by sheer willpower, because I could no longer feel my body. Of course, I started out with a burning pain in my legs, arms, and core but that had all given way to numbness. I could see that my legs continued to move my body forward, but I didn't feel like I was the one controlling them anymore. My feet were hitting the ground like bricks. And I only knew this because of the vibrations ricocheting through my skeletal system, not because my muscles had any communication with my brain.

With one half of a lap left to go, I would start eyeballing the gate to the fence around the track.

"I'm gonna stop now," the voice inside my head promised my hurting body. "I'm going to walk off the track and go to the car. My dad will know where to find me. Then we'll go home."

But once I rounded the final turn, I could see the finish line.

And once I saw it, I didn't take my eyes off it.

Eyes on the prize, I kept moving.

With 75 meters to go, I was in range of my dad's voice again.

"Come on, Chrystal! You can do it!"

I leaned forward as I crossed the finish line, just edging out a girl from another team for third place.

I didn't care.

I didn't care if I was in first place or eighth place.

All I cared about was that I was done.

That, slowly, I could breathe again.

That I eventually regained control over my body.

I completed the race because I was focused on the finish.

When my legs were completely numb, I didn't want to finish.

When my lungs screamed for more oxygen, I didn't want to finish.

But something changed inside me when I focused on the finish.

⟳

Something changes when you focus on the finish.

Something shifts when you put your energy to work in a specific area of your life and do what it takes to move forward.

> Something changes when you *focus* on the finish.

Something happens when you dig deep and keep a clear view of where you're going no matter how distant or blurry and unclear that finish line might seem.

I'm not going to lie to you. I struggle with focus. For example, not long after I decide to make healthier choices with food, there always seems to be some event where something salty or sugary is calling my name. Right after I decide to start reading one book, another pops up to vie for my attention. As soon as I start looking up something I need to know on my phone, I find myself distracted by a notification that entices me away from the task at hand.

No doubt about it—living with focus can be hard.

Some people in my life do a good job of living with focus, and I can see the blessings that hail from their choice to live this way. My brother Anthony is one of those people.

Anthony is a singer and songwriter who has worked in the music industry for years doing what he loves. Recently, he started an entertainment company that produces shows, tours, and events of all sizes.

I can clearly remember my baby brother singing in the choir on Sunday mornings at church. I'm filled with amazement to see what time invested in his God-given talents has produced. Watching him all those years ago, entertainment company ownership wasn't even a thought in my mind. So I asked him recently about focus—how he's developed it and how he's kept it.

First, Anthony told me that focus always starts with a simple decision to do one thing with what you have. My brother had a decent voice, so he sang in the church choir.

Focused living always starts with a simple decision to do one thing with what you have.

Second, he decided on a direction. More than simply singing here and there as he had a chance to, he followed the bread crumbs God placed in his path. He auditioned for

a singing group in college. He sang backup for other artists for years. He figured out what it took to create his own
album, then repeated that work to create more albums.

Third, he used discernment. He kept people around him
who encouraged his focus. He sought out resources to learn
about the direction he'd chosen, and he put himself in environments that gave him great opportunities to grow.

Finally, he exercised discipline. It wasn't easy to write
songs when he didn't feel like writing. He sometimes missed
out on hanging out with friends when it was time to record in
the studio. He invested money in his projects when he might
have bought a new car, taken a trip, or moved into a bigger
apartment.

He started by doing the one thing he knew to do, and
then he focused on doing it well.

He kept choosing to focus on the finish line. One race at
a time.

⁓

If you're like me, you may look at others who seem focused
and think they must have something you don't have or know
something you don't know.

But there is not some huge secret to it. We just have to
put enough of our time and energy toward the task at hand.

When your calendar tells you it's time to study for finals,
and you are *not* feelin' it, focusing on the finish means picturing that "A" on your report card.

When you're purposing to remain a virgin, and you're
really not feelin' it, focusing on the finish line might mean

imagining the kind of wedding night you want to have with your eventual husband.

When your friends are begging you to go with them to a party where you know kids will be violating all kinds of moral and civil laws, focusing on the finish line may mean saying you have other plans.

For most of us, keeping our eyes on the finish line isn't about winning a medal. It's about turning in papers and taking tests. It's about honoring our appointment to work out with a friend. It's about taking a risk to audition for a school theater production. It's about volunteering to serve others. It's about putting one foot in front of the other on our way to the finish line.

During high school I had a job working at Target. Because the newest employees get assigned the worst shifts, I could often count on working until closing. The customers would clear out around ten and then we'd have to stay later to clean up the store. All the clothes that had been dropped on the dressing room floor, all the bananas that had been left in the jewelry department, and all the bug spray left in the meat coolers had to be re-shelved. (If you do this . . . don't. Just don't. Cuz someone has to clean up after you.)

When I'd be walking a box of diaper wipes from sporting goods back to the baby zone, I'd remind myself to keep my eyes on the prize: I was working to save money for a prom dress. And thinking about a fluffy, shiny gown that made me look like a princess was the finish line. When I'd imagine that dress, I had the energy to slog through another shift. And another. And another.

Focusing on the finish is what propelled me to keep going.

Today I still want my choices to move me in the direction of my goals—using my gifts, honoring my marriage vows, and stewarding my health. Those decisions require discipline, sometimes more than I think I have. They also require discernment to know which people or resources can support me and how much I can engage with them.

Every single one of these areas requires focus.

Today your goals probably look a little different than mine. Maybe you want desperately to make the Varsity cheerleading team. Or maybe you have your heart set on admission to a particular Ivy League college. Maybe you want to win a poetry contest. Or maybe you want to earn enough money to send your little brother to a week of summer camp with his friends.

The good thing about focus is that it's available to anyone, anywhere.

It doesn't matter if you haven't lived a focused life up to this point. Start today. The apostle Paul says, "Brethren, I do not regard myself as having laid hold of it yet; but one thing I do: forgetting what lies behind and reaching forward to what lies ahead" (Phil. 3:13 NASB).

Choose to live with focus.

I promise you that the more you do, the clearer you will see the finish line as you move toward it.

You will have to dig deep to make decisions that are sometimes hard in order to head in a direction that sometimes seem scary, to exercise discipline that doesn't always feel good, and to use discernment to operate in an environment that can keep you from your focus.

And you will have to say no—often. So practice saying

Practice saying *no*.
Even if you have to say it to a tree. Get *good* at it.

no. Even if you have to say it to a tree. Get good at it. If you don't say no, I can guarantee that the urgent in your life will always eclipse the important.

I don't know what digging deep will look like in your life, with the decisions that you must make to honor the life of the girl in you, but I do know that you will have to focus to do it.

There is no other way.

Reflections for the Rescue

REMEMBER

Dig deep to focus on the finish.

REFLECT

- What hinders you from staying focused?
- What is the hardest part of focus for you? Making the decision, picking a direction, using discernment, or exercising discipline? How could you work on that?
- In what area of your life do you most need focus?

RESPOND

Identify one thing you need to say no to so you can say yes to the things that matter most.

HEBREWS 12:1–2; 1 CORINTHIANS 9:24–27;
2 TIMOTHY 4:7; GALATIANS 5:7; PROVERBS 4:25–27

CHAPTER 20

Left or Right?

Make good decisions

My friend Annette was a sophomore as I was starting my freshman year at Duncanville High. Because I was nervous about finding my way through a larger school campus, Annette had given me clear instructions about how to get to the spot where we'd meet each other so that she could walk me to my first period class.

When my dad dropped me off in front of the school, my instructions were simply to *turn right*.

Not exactly rocket science.

It was raining on the first day of school, and my dad stopped right in front of the flagpole, like Annette had said. He gave me a kiss on the cheek, and I stepped out of the car into the rain.

And I looked *good*. I was sporting bright blue pants that matched my blue and white paisley shirt. (Just trust me on this one. This look used to be fly. As was using the word *fly*.) My hair was straightened and sculpted into huge Shirley Temple curls. Yes . . . this was cute too.

Right in front of where my dad had dropped me off, a large throng of teens who'd flooded off buses and exited cars and locked up their bikes were like a thick stream flowing in the *opposite* direction that Annette had told me to go. And they were being sheltered from the rain more quickly than I would be if I'd turned right, taking the route less traveled. Surely if all those students were going that way, then I probably should too.

Except . . . not.

Following the crowd led me to a wing of the school I had no business being in. First, I wandered through the agriculture building, eventually winding up in woodshop.

As a result, I ended up having to trek back outside, through the rain again, until I eventually found Annette huddled under an awning in the commons, where we'd agreed to meet. It's where most of my classes would be that day.

Let's not even talk about my hair.

Sometimes we've been given all the information we need to make a good decision. But when the moment comes to make it, we may start to feel a little shaky. And our mind starts to play tricks on us.

If everyone else is going this way, then maybe . . .

My parents don't know what's up . . .

But this other way seems easier . . .

The school guidance counselor probably doesn't know what she's talking about . . .

Chances are, you already have all you need to make a good decision.

I know the pressure, as a teen, to want to fit in. We don't want to make a different decision when everyone else is doing something else. But honoring the girl inside you may require just that. It might mean acting on the decision you felt so sure about but have begun to question. It might mean sticking to that choice despite the chaotic inputs that feel confusing and overwhelming.

Seriously, make a freakin' decision. Because when you don't actively make a decision, you actually *have* decided. Making a decision is better than making no decision.

Even turning right got my curls and me out of the rain!

Yes, turning left was the wrong decision, but if I had made no decision at all—going neither to the left or the right—I might still be standing in front of the flagpole feeling awkward and confused.

Sometimes the best decision you can make is simply to make a decision.

Believe me, I say that as someone who's a bona fide overthinker and the queen of analysis paralysis. I'm the worst!

Making a decision seems simple enough, doesn't it? You have at least two choices and then you pick one, right?

Yeah, right.

If that were the case, then the road of life wouldn't be marked with flat squirrels who couldn't make a decision.

The problem for most of us is not about *making* a decision, it's about making a decision that results in *action*. Yet results come only when we take action. We have to move from thinking about it to doing something about it.

Recently, I met a lifelong friend for coffee to catch up. After a while of what I like to call chick-chat, it was time to do what I enjoy doing most: ask questions.

I asked my friend how she was really doing. I asked about her dating life, her work life, her spiritual life, and her emotional well-being. I asked her if she felt she was doing everything she could to maximize the life she had and if she was enjoying the benefits of a satisfied soul.

She said no.

When I prodded a bit, I learned that the main source of her struggle was that she hadn't been pursuing a dream of hers. She was clear on the goal but overwhelmed when it came to taking action. Inundated by more choices than she knew what to do with, she had done nothing.

So I asked her a few questions to help her move from desire to decision.

What was one thing she could do today to get the ball rolling? Was there a phone call she could make or a website she could review? Did she need to set up a meeting, make more time in her schedule, or remove a commitment to create room for a new one?

Some decision is better than no decision even if the decision you make today is small.

> *Some* decision is better than no decision even if the decision you can make today is *small*.

I know you're facing a host of decisions during this season of your life.

Choosing what electives to take can feel really huge.

Deciding whether to stop after two years of a foreign language or whether to continue for a third can be a dilemma.

Knowing whether or not to join the school club that meets twice a week might feel overwhelming.

Choosing between a pricy college that's offered a little scholarship money and a less expensive school that hasn't offered aid might be paralyzing.

Deciding whether to obey your parents' guidance and direction, when you really, *really* want to ignore them and do what you want to do might tug at your insides.

Wrestling with whether to be a person of integrity and character at your job—when others are texting friends and slipping inventory into their purses—is a choice that requires guts.

Sometimes you'll be facing a choice or a change that's so big you have to break it down into smaller parts. As my aunt challenged me: do what you can with what you have.

Packing for summer camp or for college? Pack one box.

The cost of college is daunting for your family? Set aside something from every paycheck you earn.

A habit of praying fervently seems unattainable? Pray one prayer right now.

The relationship you need to end may threaten to rip your heart out? Write down the words you need to say and practice speaking them out loud.

I'm convinced that the enemy of good decision-making is the inability or unwillingness to nail desires down to a next step. Desires become decisions when they are connected to an action.

Desires become decisions when they are connected to an *action*.

When we were growing up, my sister Priscilla participated in gymnastics, and she was one of the better gymnasts in her class. She was also the only black gymnast.

One weekend, the girls at the gym organized a team party—and my sister was not invited. That stinks, right? We've all had that feeling of being left out at one time or another.

But wait, it's not over yet. It's about to get rougher.

Somehow my mom found out about the party, and she took my sister to it anyway!

Can you imagine what it took for my sister to walk into that home?

Courage. Lots of courage.

But she made up her mind that she wasn't going to let other people's petty opinions of her determine how she lived.

And on Monday she showed up at the gym, kept giving 100 percent, and ended up taking home a bunch of awards that season.

She made a decision to be true to herself and she acted on it.

Habakkuk 2:2 offers some clues about making good decisions: "Write a vision, and make it plain so that a runner can read it" (CEB).

Based on this Bible verse, let me give you three steps

to making a decision with your desired destination clearly in mind.

Step 1: Write It Down

A businessman named Lee Iacocca once said, "The discipline of writing something down is the first step toward making it happen."[6] It's a proven fact that writing things down makes them more likely to happen.

When God gave a vision to Habakkuk, He also told him to write it down. God knows that we are quick to be inspired, but often slow to take action. When God gave the Ten Commandments to Moses, he had Moses write them down. In Revelation, when John experienced a vision of heaven, God told him to write down what he saw. God knows we are notorious for getting distracted and forgetting to live with the end in mind.

When you write down the desires of your heart and the destination you hope to reach, you clarify your thoughts and reinforce your intentions for tomorrow based on aspirations you hold today.

Step 2: Remember It

Don't forget to keep your vision in plain sight. If you write down your desires and stick them in the side pocket of your purse to make friends with forgotten pieces of gum, loose change, or old lipstick, those desires will not be front and center in your mind or heart.

Write them down and put them somewhere you will

see them. In your car. At your desk. As a reminder on your phone. Lipstick or Expo marker on your bathroom mirror will work too.

And look at it as often as possible so you never forget your destination.

Step 3: Rehearse It

Habakkuk was told to write the vision and make it plain so somebody else would know about the end game as well.

Something happens when you choose to share your destination with someone else. A friend of mine puts it this way: When you share your vision with someone else, you give it oxygen. And isn't that what we all need—a little room to breathe and believe that change is possible?

Now, pick something. Don't stress. Don't overanalyze. Don't wait for the perfect time.

Remember, the first key to living with focus is to make decisions that lead to actions—even small ones—that align with your aspirations.

So seal your decision.

Act.

Now.

Reflections for the Rescue

REMEMBER

Sometimes the best decision you can
make is simply to make a decision.

REFLECT

- How have you seen analysis paralysis in your life?
  What has analysis paralysis prevented you from
  accomplishing?
- Where in your life do you need to make a
  decision?
- Why do you think that decision has been hard to
  make?

RESPOND

Challenge yourself to make some small decision today.
Solidify that decision by writing it down, putting it in a
place where you can see it, and then pick up the phone
and share it with someone else for accountability.

PHILIPPIANS 3:13; HABAKKUK 2:2;
PROVERBS 3:4–6; JOSHUA 24:15; DEUTERONOMY 30:15;
PSALM 119:10–16; REVELATION 2:5

CHAPTER 21.

Don't Miss Your Exit

Maintain your direction by paying attention

W hen I was fifteen I took driver's education, and when I was sixteen I got my driver's license.

If you haven't gotten your driver's license yet, you'll probably be working toward it in the next few years.

In Texas, where I grew up and where my kids are growing up, drivers are no longer eligible to be fully licensed at sixteen. They can earn a *provisional* license at age sixteen—limiting the hours they can drive, and the people who can be in the car—but they don't get their full license until they are eighteen. Part of the provisional license says that you can't drive with more than one passenger under the age of twenty-one who isn't a family member.

The powers that be who are responsible for licensing drivers realized that teenage drivers are still mastering the art of paying attention. It's no secret that when you get a few friends in the car, it gets harder to focus on the road. I'm not even throwing shade; it's just how it is. One friend will tell an engrossing story about what she saw someone else's boyfriend doing last weekend. Another friend reaches for the dashboard to turn on her favorite radio station. Another insists that everyone look at the ridiculous meme on her phone. And the friend in the way, way back keeps begging for more air-conditioning. It's fair to say that the driver's mind is most certainly going to be on matters *other* than the road.

The very best drivers are those who are alert to and aware of what's happening around them. They notice that semi truck swerving slightly. They notice the goat riding in the front seat of that Volkswagen beetle. They use their signals to let other drivers know when they're heading for the exit ramp in search of a chocolate shake. They also notice the signs that can help them navigate their course.

When you're distracted, you miss the sign warning you that a speed bump is ahead.

When you're distracted, you miss the sign directing you to take the next exit for your destination.

And when you're really distracted, you see the sign and *still* miss your exit.

Although you might not see reflective yellow triangles or shiny red octagons, there are signs for you to notice on your journey to becoming the woman God made you to be.

Did you look forward to that summer internship where you got to work as an assistant to an entrepreneur or dread it?

Did you visit a special nursing home resident on your own time or fake being sick so you didn't have to go with the youth group?

Did you stay up late at night sketching costume designs for your school's spring musical, or did you race out the door the second costume design meetings ended?

Did you discover a passion for building architectural models or did the program cool your interest in becoming an architect?

Paying attention to what you're experiencing right now—whether it's babysitting, helping a neighbor garden, improving your time in the 400, or solving math equations—offers valuable signals to where you're heading, who you're becoming, and when you need a course correction.

Notice what you look forward to, what brings you joy, what you want to be doing in your free time, and what makes you lose track of time—in a good way. Also notice what you dread, what saps your energy, what you try to avoid, and when you're counting the minutes for something to end!

Pay attention.

It's that simple.

So if staying on track simply requires paying attention, why is staying on track so hard?

Because it's so easy to get distracted.

A lot of girls I knew in high school behaved as if their choices and decisions and self-awareness didn't impact their future. I remember one girl who was sweet, beautiful, and smart—but had a reputation for sleeping around. Another girl had a major potty mouth. One girl I ate lunch with always seemed to be on the verge of failing a class—and didn't seem to care. She almost bragged about her failures. I didn't get it. They were definitely focused on finishing high school and getting to college, but they didn't have a vision to explore who they would be beyond that.

Is what you're doing today going to get you where you want to be tomorrow?

What bumps and inclines and potholes and green lights are right in front of you? I also want to encourage you to intentionally look ahead to what might be on the horizon.

There is one problem, though.

Paying attention takes effort.

Self-evaluation takes time and careful scrutiny.

Most of us don't practice paying attention to our lives. Paying attention is different from simply looking at your life and making an initial assessment or a correction. Paying attention should be a habit. Consistent. Regular. Practice. How else will you stay aware and in touch with your life? This habit helps you to stick with corrections you make and to stay on track.

> Paying *attention* should be a *habit*. Consistent. Regular. Practice.

Proverbs 4:23 says, "Watch over your heart with all diligence, for from it flow the springs of life" (NASB).

To nurture the person you want to be, you have to fight to take notice of your soul and to guard the place from which you live. With diligence. That means continuous effort, conscientiousness, and hard work.

Do you get it?

This journey to honor your girl is going to require your participation.

Most of us are aware that things can drift off course if we don't stay on top of them. That's why we go to the doctor for well-visits, the dentist for checkups, and the salon for haircuts. That's why we clean out closets when clothes go out of style (or we can't fit into them anymore). That's why your mom asks you to do the dishes every night. That's why when you own a car, you need to change the oil, rotate the tires, and service the brakes. It requires maintenance. Every now and again you have to look—or have someone else look—at your car to see how well it's working.

To live with focus, we need to be willing to do the work of paying attention to our souls with the same diligence we pay attention to other areas of our lives.

Allow me to share with you three simple ways to pay attention to your life.

First, take time to review. Remember when I told you to write down the decisions you make? Well, when you do, you get to see your progress! But only if you regularly review your written intentions.

Last year, I noticed I wasn't doing a good job of telling the people in my life that I love them. I felt it. Many times I

Regularly review your written *intentions*.

showed it. But I wasn't saying it. Since I think it's important to say those words every now and again, I decided to make my I-love-yous an area of focus for the next ninety days.

So I wrote the words "Say I Love You" in a little notebook I carried around with me, and as I spoke those words, I wrote down to whom I said them. Seeing that written reminder helped me pay attention, and paying attention helped me make a change that mattered to me.

Every time I said the words, I'd smile, and a warm feeling would rise up on the inside because I knew I'd done something good in the world that day. After a while, I experienced great joy in seeing how far I'd come in being the person I wanted to be.

Write down your decisions and, every now and then, review your progress.

Second, make time to retreat. When I was your age, I had no idea how valuable it was to pause.

Stop.

Renew.

Regroup.

Maybe you've never considered it but leaving margin in your life for reflection can benefit you in ways you've not yet imagined. Create time in your schedule to be still, to be quiet, and to be alone.

If you always drive your car with music blasting, you might miss sounds coming from your engine that can tell you something under the hood isn't right.

If you are watching yet another episode of *Keeping Up with the Kardashians* or *American Ninja Warrior*, why don't you turn off the TV and have a conversation that matters with someone in your real life?

If you fall asleep at night with your hot glowing phone in your hand, consider shutting it off thirty minutes before bedtime and journaling about your day before you conk out.

Look at your schedule and pencil in non-negotiable time for you to hear yourself think, feel the rhythm of your soul, and see your life from an objective angle. Don't be legalistic about it. Just be intentional.

And as you contemplate your plan for pulling away, don't forget prayer. Jesus himself had three years to teach, train the disciples, and then die to save the world, yet He unapologetically withdrew from people to pray. If Jesus needed to break away to pray, then surely we do too. Look at your schedule and carve out space to spend time with God.

Leave margin in your life for *reflection*.

Third, go to sleep! Does that sound too much like your mom? I hear it, I do. But you know it's because I want the best for you, right? (If you are already committed to sleeping in late and taking naps, this reminder isn't for you.) Rest gives you the clarity and capacity to be fully present. And remember, even God rested on the seventh day.

People who have long-term success with their physical, emotional, and spiritual lives have learned to live attentively.

Yes, paying attention takes effort, but you *can* develop the habit. And as you do, you will also start plugging in to your potential and realizing that you can nurture and honor the girl in you.

Reflections for the Rescue

REMEMBER

Practice the art of paying attention.

REFLECT

- In what area of your life do you tend to drift off course?
- How do you know when you are drifting?
- How can paying attention to your life help you focus and stay on track?

RESPOND

What tip for paying attention resonates most with you? How will you use that tip in your day-to-day life? Think about your answer. Then write it down.

EPHESIANS 6:18; 1 CORINTHIANS 16:13; PROVERBS 4:23; PSALM 32:8; JEREMIAH 29:13; PSALM 19:14; 1 PETER 5:8–9

CHAPTER 22

Heed Those Warning Bells

Use discernment

One Friday I spent much of my day at school strategizing the best way to convince my parents to let me go to a school basketball game. I was fifteen and in ninth grade. In the end, I opted for good old-fashioned begging, beginning the second I got home from school.

"Please, Mom?" I pressed. "Pretty please? Candace can drive me, so you don't even have to worry about that."

I need to clarify that I did not have permissive parents. They weren't my "friends," like some hip parents try to be. In my family, parents were parents, and kids were kids. I knew my folks expected to know the friends I was with and, because my parents hadn't met Candace yet, I assumed my mom wouldn't let me go.

Handing me a plate with some sliced apples and peanut butter on it, my mom looked me in the eye and said, "I'll leave it up to you."

I couldn't have been more surprised if she gave me the keys to the car and told me to have fun in Mexico for the weekend.

Until that point not a lot of the significant choices in my life had been left up to me. Because my parents had made most of my big decisions, I felt the weight of being given the sudden and surprising autonomy to make one.

The ball was in my court.

As I considered it, I realized there was a reason my other friends hadn't met Candace. Let's just say she was a little rougher around the edges than my friends from the private middle school. I'd secretly suspected they wouldn't approve.

After some soul-searching, something in my gut just wasn't settled about going out with Candace. After an hour or so, I made the difficult decision not to go to the game. Even though the choice had been mine, I felt disappointed and a little grumpy. Okay . . . a *lot* grumpy.

On Monday morning I learned that Candace had gotten into a fight with another girl after Friday's basketball game and had been suspended from school.

Although it hadn't been an easy choice to skip the game, I realized that—because I'd paid attention to that feeling in my gut—my discernment had been right on the mark. I learned that I was capable of making good decisions.

You are too.

That faithful internal radar didn't always keep me from making poor choices. Well, that's not fair. It did its job by sending me the warning signals. I just didn't always heed them.

One Saturday night, a school social was happening at the same time as a party I really wanted to go to. All the cool kids were going to be at that party, and everyone else was going to be at the school social. I knew where I wanted to be, but I also knew my parents would never—in a million-bazillion years—let me go. I was much more certain about this than I'd been about the basketball game. This was not one of those situations where they were going to let me make my own decision.

When they dropped me off at school, I surveyed the crowd and, as expected, all the cool kids were absent.

I hadn't been there long when a few guy friends stopped by the school gym and offered me a ride to the party.

Had there been a soundtrack to that evening, the audience would have heard the ringing of the alarm and seen the flashing red warning lights. I felt it in my gut, but I ignored it. As I slid into the backseat of the car, I remember thinking, *This is not a good idea.*

But I wanted to go *soooo* much.

On the way to the party, we stopped to get gas. When the driver noticed a police car nearby, he whispered to his friend, "I hope they don't look in our trunk."

Curious, I asked, "What's in the trunk?"

The driver answered, coolly, "A couple of six-packs."

While I nodded like I was down with that, my insides were screaming, "I'M GONNA GO TO JAIL!"

While I now know that would be highly unlikely, it felt like a very real possibility in that moment.

When we got to the party, something didn't feel quite right—I mean besides lots of underage kids drinking beer—but I struggled to name it. I felt anxious, and I started checking in to find the first car that would be driving back to school. Between inquiries, I was praying, "Please, let me get home without getting busted. Lord, don't let me go to jail. Please don't let me be here when the police raid this party." I was suddenly very aware of the bells and whistles going off inside me, and I wanted nothing more than to heed them. Thankfully, I was able to catch a ride with a couple of girls. As I listened to them talking, I realized that what hadn't felt quite right at the party had been the smell of weed. So now there would be a drug charge added to my jail sentence.

I'd had everything I needed to make a good decision—and still chose to make a poor one. I had common sense. I had a conscience cautioning me. I even had the voices of my parents in my head, confirming what I already knew to be true.

I'd had the opportunity to exercise wise discernment. And I chose not to.

Maybe you've had moments like this.

You knew it would be smart to steer clear of a certain person.

You were aware that it was wiser to avoid a particular place.

Or you understood that refusing to buy or participate in a certain thing was the right decision.

But . . .

You ignored the warning bells.
You did what you thought would feel good.
You failed to exercise discernment.
You made a poor choice.

Maybe it's something as simple as studying for a test.

You didn't put the time into studying for it, and your grade reflected that. That's another one I learned from! After getting a little cocky about my academic abilities, I slacked off studying and ended up getting a D.

It happens, right?

But did you learn from it? Did you commit to not making that choice again?

I can assure you that I didn't end up at anymore sketchy parties in high school.

And I never slacked off in studying again.

I made lots of other mistakes, but not those two.

When I was faced with these decisions, I heard what some people call a "still, small voice" inside me. That's another way of saying that my discernment was working!

Your discernment, that voice of wisdom that helps you determine the right course of action, will work. But it will only work to the degree that you're willing to heed it. If you're willing to listen, it will help you make the best choices about the people, places, and things in your life.

That feeling in your gut is the guide God has knit inside of you. Practice discernment by listening to that feeling in your gut. He also provides guides outside of you to help you on your journey.

⤔

Surrounding yourself with the right people is a key part of discernment.

I call these key people: pacers, partners, and promoters. I recognized these important roles when I trained for and ran a marathon.

A pacer is the person who runs with a sign displaying their pace to let other runners know exactly how fast they're going. If you keep the pacer in view, they'll keep you focused on the speed you need to go.

Although she never signed up for the assignment, my friend Annette was a pacer for me. One year older than me, I watched the choices Annette made. She pushed herself to take challenging classes. She worked hard in band to make first chair in flute. When I needed a study buddy, I could count on her. Annette didn't seem overly concerned about trying to fit in. Instead, she was confident and content with doing Annette.

A partner is that person in the trenches with you, working to accomplish a goal you both share. While training for my marathon, a dear friend and I came alongside each other for mutual encouragement, accountability, and company.

A person who was a partner in my journey was Candi, a friend in the same grade. We were both committed to taking honors classes, making good grades, and seeking college scholarships. Today Candi is the vice president of an entertainment company. We both had high standards and championed each other in reaching for our goals and dreams.

And finally, there is the promoter. The person who encourages you and provides support. The friend who shows up at a race to cheer you along at the finish line. Promoters campaign on your behalf.

A teacher who I'll call Mrs. Madison was my promoter. She was my last class of the day during my junior year, and I'd hang out with her after school. The class I was taking from her, Econ and Government, was hard and I was struggling in it. I started showing up because I wanted to do better in her class, and she ended up giving me invaluable study skills I went on to use in all my classes.

Surround yourself with people who get where you're trying to go—people who can support you, join you, or give you some direction. If some people in your life don't do any of the above, it's your job to decide the amount of influence they have in your life—or whether they should be in your life at all.

Yes. It's that serious.

The people we allow in our lives can build us up, encourage us to be faithful, and help us follow through on the decisions we've made and the direction we've chosen, especially when we don't feel like sticking with the training plan.

If you're serious about doing the work of moving forward, you need people in your life who are serious about seeing you move forward too.

Be deliberate about the choices you make regarding the people in your life.

If you're serious about doing the work of moving forward, you need people in your life who are serious about seeing you move forward too.

It never ceases to amaze me how many people will complain about what they don't have, yet they don't position themselves to get it. Your environment matters. The places and spaces where you do life can propel you forward into more of the life you want if you are willing to make the adjustments. When we choose environments—and people—that support our efforts, it becomes easier to do what we need to do.

If you're in real need of community—with people who can surround you as you do the work of honoring the life God has given you—are you putting yourself in places where you will find the community you desire?

My oldest daughter and her husband are photographers. They started out doing graduation photos, family portraits, and some weddings here and there. Then they decided they wanted to increase their photography business by doing more weddings. So they started going to wedding expos. Lots of them. Just by virtue of being in that particular place, they got exposure to other people in the wedding industry and made connections. Ultimately, their business exploded as a result of positioning themselves in the right place.

When I was in middle school and high school, youth group was an important part of my life. Being committed to that community in my church formed me.

When I was struggling with loneliness and having a regular quiet time, joining a weekly Bible study in my area met both my need for community and my need for consistency in the Word.

If you want to grow spiritually, attend church or a Bible study.

If you want to avoid drugs and alcohol, make weekend plans with friends to do something other than go to parties.

Align your environment with your *ambitions*.

If you want to be accepted to the college of your dreams, meet up with friends at the library instead of vegging out on someone's couch staring at your phones.

Align your environment with your ambitions.

Just last night, I saw a commercial for *American Ninja Warrior*, where contestants compete on obstacle courses. (Yes, I do watch this show and other reality TV *sometimes*.) What got my attention was that the commercial focused on a competitor who was wearing a prosthetic. He was going to compete with one leg.

The statement he made during that thirty-second spot has resonated in my head: "I had cancer. The only way to save my life was to cut off my leg."

The commercial then cut away to scenes from the show where he is maneuvering the course with one leg less than everyone else.

But he was alive to do it.

He decided that if what was attached to him would stop him from living—even if it was a limb—he would have to let that thing go.

Every day, we're bombarded with things. Things to buy. Things to do. Things to watch. Things to read. Things to know. If we aren't careful, those things can suck the life right out of us. It's your job to make sure nothing gets in the way of living the way you're meant to live.

Sometimes we have to let go of what's killing us, even if it's killing us to let go.

Are you spending your allowance and paycheck at the mall instead of saving for a computer for college? Is your addiction to social media robbing you of time to do something productive? Are you buying Starbucks five-dollar

> Sometimes we have to *let go* of what's killing us, even if it's *killing us* to let go.

lattes every morning on the way to school? What *things* are infecting or affecting your precious and rare life?

Who do you want to be? What do you want to do? Where do you want to go?

Yes, you must be diligent to make a decision. Yes, you must pay attention so you maintain your direction. And yes, you must exercise discernment in selecting the people, places, and things that can help and support you on your way. When it comes to your heart, your mind, your soul, and your body, be a ruthless gatekeeper who protects against anything that will take from your life or interfere with your discernment.

Discernment is the rudder that will get you where you're going.

Reflections for the Rescue

REMEMBER

Align your environment with your ambitions.

REFLECT

- Who supports you, joins you, or gives you direction?
- Who keeps you from making the best choices?
- Who are *you* supporting, joining, or giving direction to?

RESPOND

Take a piece of paper and make two columns. On one side write "Good Discernment" and list the people who represent good discernment on your part. On the other side write "Poor Discernment" and list the people who illustrate your need to use more discernment in your life. Now pick something off the "Poor Discernment" side of the paper and decide what you can do to let that person go.

———— ✖ ————

1 CORINTHIANS 9:24; HEBREWS 12:1;
PROVERBS 27:17; PROVERBS 17:17; HEBREWS
10:24–25; ROMANS 12:4–5; ROMANS 16:17

CHAPTER 23

What My Marathon Taught Me

Exercise discipline

I have always struggled with tardiness.

And while I'd love to pretend it's because my life is so full right now *and* because I'm juggling an awful lot of balls *and* because I'm so super-duper important, that's just not the case. I mean, those things are true, but I can't blame my tardiness on them.

When I was sixteen and worked at Target, let's just say I struggled to show up to work on time and punch my time card.

When I was seventeen and worked as a secretary for a chiropractor, well, I rarely made it to the office by nine a.m. The job was a thirty-minute drive from our house, and time after time, I showed up just a *little bit* late. It was almost as if my brain wouldn't let me get there on time.

When I was in my twenties though, working in customer

service, my tardiness finally caught up with me. I lost a job because of it.

Though it's a little embarrassing to admit, I want you to know it.

Whether you acknowledge it or not, you are practicing *now* who you'll be *later*. What that means is that you need to begin doing *now* what will be expected of you *then*.

Do it whether you want to or not.

That's what discipline is. It's doing something because you've decided to do it whether you feel like it or not.

It might feel tempting to put off as much responsibility as possible until you're older, when you decide you're finally a "real" adult. The reason I want to caution you against operating that way, besides the threat of losing a good job, is because only one person is going travel from this season to the next one with you—and that's *you*. And while you certainly can choose to put off exercising discipline, those poor habits are going to be a lot harder to fix later on.

Don't ask me how I know.

I know.

What you do today has ramifications on what you will do tomorrow.

Be a good student today because you want to be a person who does well on the job tomorrow. Trust me on this. You want to have a job you like. You will spend a lot of your life working.

Be discerning about whom you spend time with now because there's this very true saying, "Show me your friends and I can show you your future."

Treat your body with respect because today's body *is* tomorrow's body.

Listen to your parents. For real. L-I-S-T-E-N to what they have to say today, or you'll be asking them how to clean up your mess tomorrow.

Discipline today opens up possibilities for tomorrow.

One of my favorite movies of all time is *The Great Debaters*. Denzel Washington is in it. Need I say more? He stars along with other great actors in a story set in the 1930s in the middle of the Jim Crow South. The film is based on the true story of Melvin Tolson, a professor at Wiley College in Texas. Mr. Tolson formed the school's first debate team, which enjoyed great success competing against the country's top schools and eventually against Harvard in a national championship.

At one point in the movie, one of the debaters expresses his frustration to his father about the amount of work required to compete on the debate team. He laments the large investment of time, the difficulty of the preparation, and the pressure from Mr. Tolson.

The father, an educator himself, looks his son in the eye and delivers what, to me, is *the* line of the movie: "Son, we do what we *have* to do so we can do what we *want* to do."[7]

Bam.

Drop the mic.

Really, the movie could have ended right then.

But it didn't.

The film continued to illustrate what happened when the young students chose to embody the wisdom of those words and exercise discipline—doing what they didn't feel

like doing much of the time. It also illustrated so beautifully what it looked like for those kids to know victory.

Most of us can exercise some form of self-discipline when we need to.

> We do our chores.
> We practice our instruments.
> We practice with our sports teams.
> We obey the law—sometimes. (Speed limits can be a problem for me.)
> We don't say the first thing that comes to mind—most of the time.

Discipline is more than motivation. Discipline pushes past the desire to quit when motivation runs out.

Just trust me on this.

When I was dating in high school, I knew that healthy boundaries were important, but I didn't feel like setting them.

When I struggled with perpetual tardiness in my twenties,

Discipline is more than motivation. Discipline pushes past the desire to quit when *motivation runs out.*

I knew being late might get me fired, but when the alarm went off, I didn't feel like getting up.

When I desire deep fellowship with God, I know meeting with Him daily is the key to staying connected, but there are times when I feel like spending a few more minutes on social media more than I feel like carving out time with Him.

Motivation fluctuates or runs out because it's based on how we feel. Have you noticed that our feelings change constantly?

Discipline is the habit of acting in the moment based on a decision you made ahead of time, regardless of your feelings. Discipline is the action that bridges the gap between your dreams and your reality.

Discipline is the sinew that connects your decision, your direction, and the discernment you must use each and every day. It binds you by your will—not your emotions or circumstances.

Most importantly, discipline is what gets you going again when you've screwed up, dropped the ball, or gotten off course. It compels you to move forward over and over.

> Discipline *binds* you by your *will*—not your emotions.

Why did I decide to run a marathon? I don't know.

To this day, I think it's one of the dumbest things I've ever done.

In high school I'd wanted to run the shorter races and

was disappointed to be slated for longer ones. And now I registered to run a marathon? On purpose?

I think I signed up for the marathon because I'd had one brief moment of glory after a successful three-or four-mile run and thought I was marathon material. It's funny the games your brain will play in a few seconds of endorphin-inspired motivation. For a few moments, I thought I was an athlete, and I decided I was capable of running 26.2 miles if I put my mind to it.

A few months later, when I found myself dreading each long Saturday run, I kept working at my goal. Why? Because I was invested. Because I'd told friends, family, and basically everybody via social media that I was going to do it. Because I had committed. Because I wanted that medal.

But looking back, I realize there was more to it.

Little by little, with each Saturday run, I was exercising discipline—showing up, doing the work, regardless of how I felt. Sometimes the thread of commitment is all that keeps us connected to our goals.

As the runs got longer and harder, as much as I wanted to skip runs here and there, I did them anyway. I had developed the habit of doing what I didn't feel like doing, and that habit helped me stick with my decision.

That same habit of discipline didn't just help me prepare for my race; it helped me finish it.

A few months later, my finish looked nothing like I'd envisioned. It was quite depressing. It rained. I clocked my slowest pace ever. My rocking marathon playlist was of no use when my phone got wet and died with ten miles still to go. When I finally crossed the finish line, very few people were still there.

Can I be honest? Initially, it was a bit deflating. My expectations of what the finish would look like were not met—at all. But that's not the whole story.

I remember the slow realization of something important. I had crossed the finish line. I'd had a goal. And I'd finished. Sweaty, stinky, tired, and sore, I'd accomplished what I'd set out to do. I made my dream a reality. I'd run my race.

What is your finish line?

Is it academic fulfillment, physical health, or spiritual growth and maturity?

The commitment to cross the finish line you choose doesn't start tomorrow. It starts today.

You practice. You show up. You work at it.

You operate with priorities. You put first things first.

And then you do it again.

And again.

✎

Discipline requires doing what you *have to* do so you can do what you *want to* do.

Want to be ready for the man of your dreams? You *have to* stop wasting time and sharing your soul with the guys who aren't.

Want to have a life filled with passion and purpose? You

> Discipline requires doing what you *have to* do so you can do what you *want to* do.

have to spend time following the instructions He's already provided.

Want to know God's will for your life? You *have to* take the small opportunities you have right now to use the gifts He has given you.

Luke 16:10 says, "If you are faithful in little things, you will be faithful in large ones. But if you are dishonest in little things, you won't be honest with greater responsibilities" (NLT).

When I realize that I need to work on discipline in spending time with the Lord, the first task at hand is to wake up early. I look at my bedtime routine to make sure I'm setting myself up for success to get up when that alarm goes off. I also build in rewards that motivate me in other ways. I love hot tea, so when I wake up I make my way to the kitchen, heat up the water, and grab a peppermint tea bag. Another thing that fills me up is coffeehouse music, so I find some on Spotify and pipe it through the speakers.

Now I'm ready. With peppermint tea in hand and coffeehouse music in the background, I crack open my Bible to read and be nourished in the Word.

Discipline isn't easy, but it's necessary. It takes reprogramming your habits and your thoughts, as well as mastering

The *discipline* with which you live will be the *foundation* on which you create a life you love.

your emotions. The discipline with which you live will be the foundation on which you create a life you love. Discipline isn't easy, but it's worth it.

Do what you *have to* do now, so you can do what you *want to* do later.

Reflections for the Rescue

REMEMBER

The discipline with which you live is the foundation
on which you create a life that you love.

REFLECT

- Have you ever had a goal that you gave up on
  because of how you felt?
- Where in your life do you have discipline? Where
  do you lack discipline?
- If discipline is the vehicle through which you
  accomplish your goals, habits are the tracks on
  which discipline runs. What habits in your life need
  to be broken? What habits do you need to build?

RESPOND

Discipline is based on actions you do whether you feel
like doing them or not. Think of one small task that you
have been avoiding. Get up and do it. Practice makes
perfect. Discipline is a muscle that you can build.

**1 TIMOTHY 4:7; ROMANS 13:14; DANIEL 1:8; TITUS 2:12;
HEBREWS 5:11–14; 1 CORINTHIANS 9:25–27; HEBREWS 12:11;
PROVERBS 12:24; PROVERBS 20:13; PROVERBS 25:28**

CHAPTER 24

Doing the Next Thing

Just keep going

While my friend Shelly was in nursing school, a friend of hers, one of her fellow students, was diagnosed with a brain tumor. I'll call her Beth.

I'll be honest: I have no idea what I would do if I were in Beth's situation. Would I drop out of school? Maybe. Would I ask my mom to move in and take care of me? Maybe. Would I curl up in a ball and cry for days? Likely.

Shelly watched Beth do something very different. When she had brain surgery, Beth took a semester off from school to focus on her health and recovery. But then Beth returned to classes and continued her studies in nursing. Beth wanted to become a nurse, and she didn't allow her illness to divert her from the path she saw ahead of her.

Beth persisted. She committed to moving forward toward her goals. She reminds me of Nemo's friend Dory who relentlessly chanted, "Just keep swimming."

Making some progress toward our goals is often the

very thing that jacks most of us up. We make the connection. We experience the moment of motivation. We feel the joy of a soul set on fire. We decide to do something about the pain.

We start.

We take one step, maybe even two.

But we don't keep going.

How do I know? Because I've done it a few times.

Motivated, inspired, or stimulated by some talk I heard, some book I read, some person I met, or some place I went, I started out strong. But then—when things got difficult or boring—I quit.

I stopped swimming.

As a single mom in my early twenties, I'd settled for living from paycheck to paycheck. I wasn't aspiring to be or do any more than make ends meet. It took me a minute to realize this, but after disappointing myself a few times, I started working toward a brighter future again.

When we head in a new direction, begin a new journey, or travel someplace unknown or uncharted, there's always a level of discomfort. The experience can be uncomfortable.

Unanticipated.

Unsettling.

When we find ourselves on a long road with less light than we'd like, we may doubt our decision to begin in the first place. Or we simply don't exercise the discipline to stick with the voyage.

And this place, my friend, is where many of us abandon the adventure of truly living. Most of us don't like traveling in the dark. We prefer not to stay in places where we feel uneasy. We don't want things to be hard.

So we doubt.

We hesitate.

We give up.

We decide not to embrace the long winding path, the labor of loving God's image in us.

We pull into an unfamiliar driveway, turn around, and go home.

Again.

Can I just stop right here and tell you that I've stopped and started over more times in my life than I care to admit? Nobody wants to be uncomfortable, including me. There have been times that, while I felt drawn to the girl I could be, the journey required more of the right-now-me than I wanted to give.

So I quit.

I stayed in the relationship way too long. I didn't want to be lonely. I quit on making good decisions for me.

I spent more money on right now rather than saving for later. I didn't want to wait.

I started reading through the Bible but didn't finish. I slept in late or went to bed early.

I chose healthier foods and activities—for a hot second. I skipped the salad and went straight for the chocolate.

Sound familiar?

Is there a discomfort or difficulty that got in the way of you moving farther on your journey?

If you avoid productive discomfort, you'll only be distracted and delayed from arriving at your desired destination. If you sidestep the discomfort now, you might also sidestep the peace and joy you hope for later.

Do what you can with what you have to move in that direction.

Then keep moving.

Every journey is a process. The key is to start and then keep going because every journey takes time. To live fully you must be willing to go with whatever light you have, to trust the process, and believe that God knows what he's doing with you.

My mother has always told me, "When you don't know what you are supposed to do next, just continue doing whatever God told you to do last."

The key to your journey is to start and then keep going.

Did God tell you to spend more time with Him? Keep doing it.

Did God tell you to pursue your education? Keep doing it.

Did God tell you to honor Him with your body? Keep doing it.

Did God tell you to love those who seem unlikely? Keep doing it.

Do what you know how to do.

Your decision to do what you can with what you have is how you will make real, lasting progress.

God has given you everything you need for your life. But He will not live it for you. You have to participate.

God has *given* you everything you *need* to live your *life*. But He will not live it for you.

People ask me all the time how I've made it through difficult seasons. They wonder what secrets I have to share for surviving hurt, heartbreak, and heavy loads. They want me to tell them how I function on days when it's hard to go one more step or one more mile, or to hold fast to hope after yet another disappointment.

Here's what I've done.

I've kept swimming.

I've done the next thing.

I've done what I could with what I had.

You can too.

⁓

A young widow, Ruth did the next thing, and then kept doing the next thing. Motivated by love for her mother-in-law, a heart to do the right thing, and a desire to know the God of the Israelites, she left her home, faced an unknown future, and took a chance on finding a new life while leaving behind her familiar life. She found a new love and a new purpose, and this woman found herself right smack-dab in the lineage of Christ.

An orphan, Esther did the next thing, and then kept doing

the next thing. Motivated by a love for her people, respect for wise counsel, and the recognition that her opportunity also came with responsibility, she risked a life of luxury and royalty for the survival of an entire race. Esther solidified her place in the palace and in history as a woman of power— soft, strong, shrewd, and graceful.

A prostitute, Rahab realized she had a chance to save herself from the life she'd created when one day she invited men into her home—not to service them but to serve their cause and their God. Motivated by a hope for more, a healthy fear of the Israelite God, and a will to survive impending disaster, she took the risk of a lifetime. Rahab teaches us that it's never too late, that we have never fallen too far, and that God's grace can reach anyone, anywhere, at any time. Rahab did the next thing, and then kept doing the next thing.

Do what you can now and keep doing it.

Then trust in the one who created you and gives you the strength to keep swimming.

It's never too late. We have never fallen too far. God's *grace* can reach *anyone*, anywhere, at any time.

Reflections for the Rescue

REMEMBER

The key to your journey is to start, and then to keep going.

REFLECT

- What do you know that God has told you to do?
- Have you been tempted to quit?
- What have you started that you just needed to keep working to finish? Do you know enough to go? What's getting in the way?

RESPOND

- Sometimes we don't need new information, we just need to utilize the information we already have. What do you already know that you just need to start acting on? Put a date on your next step. And do it.
- Talk to God about your desire to keep moving forward in the life He has given you. Commit to Him that you will keep moving down the road of your life.

PROVERBS 3:6; GALATIANS 6:9; HEBREWS 11:1; 2 THESSALONIANS 3:13; 2 CORINTHIANS 5:9; PHILIPPIANS 2:12–13; HEBREWS 10:36; COLOSSIANS 1:11; ROMANS 5:3–5

PART 6

ENCOURAGE
YOUR
life

CHAPTER 25

That Runaway Thought Train

Coach your head

One morning during high school I began sobbing as my dad was driving me to school.

There might possibly have been very aggressive and turbulent hormonal things happening inside my body. It would explain a lot.

I felt lonely.
I felt lost.
I felt small.
I felt frustrated.

"Chrystal," my dad asked with care and concern, "why are you crying?"

Well, that was all the permission I needed to unload all that I was carrying. And it was quite a load.

"I don't have any friends," I began.

I saw my dad's mouth open to speak.

But before my dad could get a word in, I continued, "And I'm fat!"

Before he could get a word in, I kept going.

"I don't think I'll ever do good in any of my classes. So what's the point of me even trying?"

Although I'd asked a question, I really didn't want his opinion. It was obviously a rhetorical question, so I cut him off again before he could speak.

"I probably won't succeed in life anyway!" I moaned.

Yeah, I went there. I went full misery and announced that I would probably fail. At *life*.

In another moment, I might have been able to hear the absurdity of my rant and speak truth to the madness, but in that moment, I was completely overwhelmed by my feelings.

Did I feel lonely? Yes.

Did I struggle to fit into certain groups at school? Yes.

Did I have *zero* friends? No.

As a size six, did I still dislike the shape of my body? Yes.

Were other girls size two or size four? Yes.

Was I fat? Not at all.

Was I struggling in geometry? Yes.

Do I still hate geometry to this day? Yes.

Would I never do well in any of my classes? No. Not by a long shot.

Would I fail at life? Most likely not.

I'd allowed my feelings to be the boss of me. I'd allowed my mind to run wild, and I'd blown a lot out of proportion.

What I know now that I didn't know then is that negative thinking can sabotage your present and your future. The thoughts you allow to take root in your mind can grow into weeds with real power to destroy. And that's why it's so important to eliminate them before they can grow.

I want to impress upon you the importance of cultivating a healthy thought life. If you can learn how to coach yourself to think right thoughts, you can keep moving forward.

When I started writing my last book, my excitement about both the topic and the opportunity to share it propelled me forward. (True story: the topic was the same as this book I'm writing to you! I care so much about this stuff. And about you.) I had more words than I knew what to do with, as well as tons of energy to put those words down on paper. Starting the journey was not the problem.

Eventually, I struggled with doubt, wondering if I could really help anyone, craft words worth reading, and write a book anyone would even want to finish. I felt naked and vulnerable as I ruminated on the darkness—the negativity in my mind.

Negative thinking can kill your hope, it can kill your joy, and it can kill your motivation to push past momentary problems or pressure toward the purposes God has placed in you. When you focus on thoughts that are inaccurate or fragments of the truth, those thoughts can freeze you in fear. Wrong thinking can inhibit you from moving forward.

Early on in my book-writing adventure, I came home one

day to find sticky notes posted all around my bathroom mirror. Those sticky notes stared at me each day to tell me that:

- I am a good writer.
- I am good enough.
- I am the only person who can write like me.
- My opinions and experiences matter.
- I have ideas and creativity that are worth sharing with the world.

But I didn't put those sticky notes there. My sister did.

My sister wanted to help me. She understood how important it was for me to fight the destructive thoughts that threatened to uproot what God has planted in me. She coached me.

When I looked in the mirror to wipe the matter from my eyes, I couldn't help but see messages designed to remind me of who I am and what I'm capable of accomplishing. Over and over, those words around my mirror have coached me, encouraging me to slide out from my motionless mentality, move my feet, and keep going.

Thoughts matter.

Fight the destructive thoughts that threaten to *uproot* what God has *planted* in you.

Sometimes we need help to fight the thoughts that get rooted in our minds.

When my dad and I were driving to school, and I finally got through spewing all of my negative self-talk, my dad was able to speak to the crazy.

He mentioned a few friends he'd seen me talking to.

He assured me I wasn't fat.

He reminded me that, for the most part, I was doing well in my classes.

He was even willing to venture a guess that I was going to do fine in life.

He spoke truth to the lies. He corrected my thinking. And I want you to pause to correct yours. If you don't, the thoughts you harbor will sink deeper roots into your soul.

Regardless of what is happening in your life, your thinking can either paralyze you or propel you. Proverbs 23:7 says, "For as he thinks in his heart, so is he" (AMP).

Your thoughts permeate your heart and soul and then overflow into what you do. How and what you think affects how you live. Just like how you train for a sport affects how you perform. There would have been disastrous results if I'd attempted to run the marathon without months of preparation first.

Get your thoughts out of your head by speaking them, writing them down, or sharing them with a friend. Sometimes, as soon as you express what you're thinking, you can recognize the destructive ones you've unintentionally been entertaining. Bringing your hidden thoughts out into the open is an excellent way to gain perspective on whether they are real. This is what coaches do when they review video footage from

Bringing your *hidden* thoughts out into the open is an excellent way to gain *perspective* on whether they are *real*.

a competition with their athletes. Racers, divers, gymnasts, and team players review their performances in slow-mo in order to learn and grow.

One of the best ways to examine your thoughts is to shine the light of God's truth on them instead of focusing on the monster in your mind, however real it might seem in the moment.

The goal is to take thoughts that are negative, untrue, and destructive and replace them with thoughts that are affirming, true, and constructive. You do this by renewing your mind—transforming the way you think through ongoing acceptance of right thoughts based on what God says is true. Philippians 4:8 says, "Finally, brethren, whatever is true, whatever is honorable, whatever is right, whatever is

Take thoughts that are negative, untrue, and *destructive* and replace them with thoughts that are affirming, true, and *constructive*.

pure, whatever is lovely, whatever is of good repute, if there is any excellence and if anything worthy of praise, dwell on these things" (NASB).

Let me show you how this works.

Let's say I found myself thinking this way: "I will never be able to accomplish my dreams."

That statement isn't true. You can shine the light of God's truth on that lie: "It is God who works in you to will and to act in order to fulfill his good purpose" (Phil. 2:13 NIV).

The truth is, as we follow God's direction in our lives, He is the one who will do the work in us so we can fulfill His purposes for us and the desires He has placed in us. That takes the pressure off us having to figure it all out, now, doesn't it?

Here's another one: "I am not enough. I'm not equipped. I don't belong."

The truth is if God put you where you are and if pleasing Him is your aim, then you *are* enough, you *are* equipped, and you *can* have victory over what you face. Second Corinthians 2:14 says, "But thanks be to God, who always leads us in triumph in Christ" (NASB).

You get the idea.

If you don't know the truths of Scripture, search them out. If you want to know what God thinks, discover His truth in the letter of love He's provided. He has promised that when you look for Him, you will find Him: "You will seek me and find me when you seek me with all your heart" (Jer. 29:13).

Search out the truth. Write down the verses or passages that speak to your heart, and you will change your incorrect patterns of thinking over time.

Be your own coach. Inundate yourself with the truth, and rehearse that truth so it will become a light that shines brighter than the dark thoughts that threaten to keep you from making progress. "You will know the truth, and the truth will set you free" (John 8:32).

Silence the negative thoughts. The girl in you needs to know that you believe in her. Affirm who you are, whose you are, and what is possible. Be a good coach to *yourself*.

When you choose to think and rehearse right thoughts, you battle against destructive patterns of thinking that threaten to keep the girl in you from emerging valiant and victorious. Take those destructive thoughts captive by shining the light of God's truth on them.

Reinforce your efforts by coaching yourself along the way.

Reflections for the Rescue

REMEMBER

Examine your thoughts in the light of
God's thoughts toward you.

REFLECT

- What thoughts do you have that steal your hope,
  your joy, or your motivation?
- Do you typically entertain those thoughts or fight
  back with truth? Why?

RESPOND

- The next time you struggle with entertaining a
  destructive thought, search for a Scripture on
  that topic that will shine the light of truth on the
  monster in your mind.
- Plan a good time and place to regularly get your
  thoughts out of your head. Write them down.

ROMANS 12:2; PHILIPPIANS 4:8; EPHESIANS 4:20–24;
JOHN 1:5; JOHN 8:12; 2 CORINTHIANS 10:5; JOHN 17:19

CHAPTER 26

Speak Only Truth

Coach your mouth

Michelle Carter is a world champion, an Olympic gold medalist, and an American record holder in women's shot put.

She walks out onto the field with rhythm and ease and uses her body to throw an almost nine-pound ball many meters.

It's clear that Michelle knows what she is doing.

Michelle is a friend of mine, and when she was preparing for the Olympic Games in Rio—where she won the gold medal—I asked her what it has taken for her to keep her focus and continue to have a successful career.

Michelle's response? She has learned to coach herself.

When she's on the field getting ready to throw that metal ball, she walks herself mentally through the movements she's thoroughly practiced. And she talks herself, sometimes audibly, through her game.

"Okay, girl, you know how to do this."

"Stay relaxed."

"Be patient. Don't rush it. Give your legs time to generate the power you need to throw."

Michelle understands the importance of coaching herself by being her own encourager when necessary, even if that means talking out loud to herself on the field.

∾

If you can befriend yourself and coach yourself, especially when you're weary, you will be surprised by the results.

And like any coach anywhere, your encouragement will involve using words.

Sometimes we learn how to coach ourselves by hearing and implementing the words of other coaches in our lives.

I recently heard one of my sons speaking negatively about one of his brothers. Because I'm convinced that words do matter and that they shape our perceptions of ourselves, I wasn't having it.

I interjected, "Hey, that's my son. You are not allowed to talk about my son that way."

I'm coaching my boys so that they learn how to coach themselves.

But I also hear God saying those same words when we speak poorly about ourselves.

"Hey, that's my daughter. You are not allowed to talk about my daughter that way."

The words we use—about others and about ourselves—are not spoken in a vacuum.

We agree that the words you speak about others have

the power to impact them. And we agree that the words we speak about ourselves can *form* who we are becoming. But did you know that the words you speak about *yourself* can actually impact others?

It's true.

When you make comments about being fat, you communicate to other girls and women that that's what you value. Although you never *intend* to, you undermine the value of others when you speak negatively about yourself.

When you make comments about your hair looking bad or your clothes not being together, you communicate to other girls and women that that's what you value. And although you never *intend* to, you communicate that that's the way you value them, as well.

When you make comments about your intelligence—remarking that you're "stupid" or "slow" or "dumb"—you communicate to others that you value them based on *their* intelligence.

Are you feeling me?

When you are able to accept yourself as you are, your posture of self-acceptance communicates to others that they are acceptable as they are.

For example, if you spill a strawberry smoothie on your shirt on the way to school, and don't mention it all day, you communicate to others that it's *all right* to be imperfect.

If you choose not to buy new clothes four times a year, when every new season rolls around, and decide not to talk down about the clothes you're wearing, you communicate to others that it's *all right* to dress as they choose.

If you've never had a boyfriend and refuse to speak

poorly about yourself, you communicate to others that *they* are valuable whether they have a boyfriend or not.

The way you speak *to* yourself, and the way you speak *about* yourself, has the power to infuse life and worth and value into others.

⁓

Our words matter.

Proverbs 18:21 says that "the tongue has the power of life and death."

> You will *believe* what you tell yourself, so be *careful* what you say.

You will believe what you tell yourself, so be careful what you say.

It is your job to get up every day and coach yourself, to tell yourself who you are, whose you are, and what you expect yourself to do.

Even David, the great warrior, faced times of great discouragement and difficulty. When he faced defeat at the hands of his enemies and rejection by those who claimed to be his friends, David "encouraged himself in the LORD his God" (1 Sam. 30:6 KJV).

David chose faith in the God who made him and belief in the purpose God had for his life, even when moving forward seemed hard and he felt like quitting. David encouraged himself to keep going.

Speaking life to your heart and to your situation may mean speaking God's truth out loud as you look yourself in the eye. Speaking life simply means speaking kindly to yourself and encouraging your-self just like you would a good friend. And it's worth learning to be your own best friend.

Learn to be your own best friend.

Speak kindly.

Speak with love.

And truth.

Wherever you see the need *for* change in your life, start speaking that change *into* your life. The power to do so lies in your own tongue.

You remember some of the words I said about myself in the car with my dad, right? So if you struggle to coach your mouth, I'm feeling you.

Since that day, I've learned a few things that have helped me to coach myself and refrain from using the kinds of words that will be detrimental to myself and to others.

First, I learned to avoid words like *always* and *never.*

Those words are often an over-exaggeration, so they tend to harm more than they help. For example, at home, if you're used to telling your mom that you *always* take out the garbage and your brothers *never* take out the garbage, you're actually making it harder for her to believe you! But if you're able to say, "Mom, more often than not I'm the person who's taking out the garbage. Rarely, do the boys help," you're going to have her ear. Avoid over-exaggerating in the words you use.

Second, I've learned that the negative words I say about myself can actually blind me to what is most true.

Let's say I'm stopped at a traffic light, but a big truck is in front of me. If I'm to move forward, I have to be able to see a green light. And if that truck is blocking my view, I'll never see it and I'll never move! So I either need for that truck to move or I need to find a way to see around it.

The same is true of our words.

The wise Maya Angelou said, "Words are things. You must be careful, careful about calling people out of their names, using racial pejoratives and sexual pejoratives and all that ignorance. Don't do that. Some day we'll be able to measure the power of words. I think they are things. They get on the walls. They get in your wallpaper. They get in your rugs, in your upholstery, and your clothes, and finally in to you."[8]

The negative words we speak about ourselves can actually block us from experiencing what is *more* true about us. For example, if you often joke about being lazy as an excuse for not exercising, you may not be able to see what is *more* true about you than your "laziness." If you were to choose to speak what is most true, you could look in the mirror and affirm, "God gave me this body and called it good. He also gave me the will to choose to exercise. I can take care of my body by walking to school today instead of riding the bus." You bless yourself when you speak the words that are *most* true about you.

Finally, I discovered that just because negative words were coming out of my mouth, it didn't necessarily make them true.

When we're stuck in a cycle of negative thoughts, negative self-talk is often the first to come to our mind and lips. And, yeah, it does take an effort to replace those negative

thoughts and words with positive ones. But the way you ditch the negative is to rehearse, affirm, and declare the positive. Speaking truth about your life with positive expectant hope—is key to you moving forward in a solid way.

Maybe when you look in the mirror you don't like what you see. You might find yourself saying, "I'm fat" or, "I don't like my shape." You might lament the shape of your nose, the tone of your skin, or the wave in your hair. (You know, don't you, that girls with straight hair often want curly hair and girls with curly hair often want straight hair, right? Chances are someone wants what you've got!)

But if you choose to rehearse only what's wrong with you, you'll only be putting effort into tearing yourself down. While you should do what you can to change what positively affects your health, use your words to endorse that you are a unique, beautiful creation—crooked nose, oily skin, crazy hair, and all.

Instead of saying, "I'm fat," you can say, "Every day I have the power to do something to move in the direction of a healthier version of me."

Instead of saying, "I'm ugly," you can say, "God created me exactly the way I am, and there is no other in the entire world who is like me. I am a unique and precious creation."

When I was a teen, I tried this. I won't lie: at first it didn't go well. It felt totally awkward. Seriously, my body had a visceral reaction when I tried to speak what was most true about my appearance, my intelligence, and my relationships.

I'd begin to speak the words, "I am beautiful. I am loved . . ." I couldn't keep a straight face! The first time I tried, what I saw in the mirror was me pantomiming sticking a finger down my throat and pretending to gag. I guess that's what it felt like! It was uncomfortable, and the words were getting stuck in my throat.

When I was a little kid, I despised peas. I mean I really couldn't stand them. The consistency freaked me out, and I gagged on them, unable to force them down. Eventually, I got used to them and was able to eat them without gagging and annoying everyone in my family. But I never would have gotten used to them and had the benefit of eating them, if I hadn't pushed myself to swallow them.

The true words we say about ourselves are like those peas. When we practice, when we determine to speak the truth, we're nourished and strengthened.

I want you to practice speaking what is most true about you in front of the mirror.

The first step is to "catch" or to notice, the negative words that force their way into your head and out of your mouth.

Then, replace those words with what is more true of you. Camp out there. Rehearse those lifegiving words that strengthen and nourish and build and shape who you really are.

"I am beloved by God and others."

"I have all I need to succeed."

"God made me, and my body is *good.*"

These may not be the particular words for which your soul is yearning. I encourage you to find your own true words that resonate with you and use them, encouraging and inspiring you!

Practice speaking what is most true about you in front of the mirror.

Yeah, at first it's going to feel uncomfortable, but eventually—I promise you—you'll be able to do it without gagging.

Fight for *you*.

⁓

Michelle Carter, even as an accomplished athlete, struggles with words. She used to hesitate when asked to speak in front of others because she didn't want to mess up the words, sound stupid, or not be able to express herself clearly.

The same self-coaching Michelle uses on the field has served her well when in front of a mic.

"Okay, girl, you know how to do this."

"Stay relaxed."

"Be patient. Don't rush it. Give your mind time to generate the words you want to share."

Because speaking hasn't always been comfortable for her, Michelle has learned to draw on other sources of encouragement as well.

"You may be ADD and dyslexic, but that's how God made you."

"You are worthy of this opportunity."

"You have not been given a spirit of fear."

"You can do all things through Christ who strengthens you."

Michelle rehearses what she knows to be true about herself and what she knows to be true about her God, both in her mind and with her mouth.

Be willing to encourage yourself. Even if it means being the girl who talks to herself out loud every now and then, be a good friend to *you*. Rehearse what is true and good about yourself in light of what you know to be true about the God who created you.

Reflections for the Rescue

REMEMBER

Rehearse what is true and good about yourself in light of what you know to be true about the God who created you. Silence the negative self-talk.

REFLECT

- When it comes to how you talk about yourself, do you lean to the positive or the negative? Why?
- If you were a good friend to yourself, what would you say about yourself?

RESPOND

- Think of three encouraging statements a good friend might say about you. Write those things down. Keep that list handy, and when you find yourself being more critical than supportive of yourself, use your mouth to coach yourself.
- Pick one of those statements and say it out loud, right now, to yourself.

PSALM 19:14; PSALM 141:3; PROVERBS 4:24; PROVERBS 13:3; PROVERBS 18:21; LUKE 6:45; EPHESIANS 4:29; JAMES 3:4–5

CHAPTER 27

When You're Bullied by Your Feelings

Coach your heart

Second semester of my freshman year, I called my friend Annette and she said, "Can I call you back? I'm talking to Rhonda on the other line."

"Sure," I chimed, "call me when you're done."

I said the right words, but I felt a little jealous.

The next day, after school, I saw Rhonda and Annette hop into Annette's mom's minivan.

That's when I felt more than a *little* jealous.

If you've been in a situation like this with friends, it can feel really lonely. And that's on a good day.

On most days, I felt left out.

I felt like I didn't belong.

I believed that Annette didn't care about me.

I felt like I was coming in second place. (No one made it a contest except me, mind you.)

In my mind, the situation became *very big.*

I felt like I'd lost my best friend. Somehow, when Annette had started hanging out more with Rhonda, I made up that she wasn't my friend anymore.

I was very creative and imaginative that way.

I wish I could tell you that I came to my senses after a few days, but I actually didn't talk to Annette for several months. (If you find that loco, I probably could have used you to talk some sense into me when I was in high school.)

Annette could see I was acting weird, but she had no idea why I'd stopped talking to her.

Being pummeled by my feelings felt like being at the beach when a huge inescapable wave breaks over you, thrashing you in the water, pounding you into the sand. After those months of emotional turbulence, I wrote Annette a long letter.

It began,

"Dear Annette, I feel really sad that you don't want to be my best friend anymore . . ."

Pouring my emotions onto the page—like that vomiting emoji spewing green slime—I let Annette know how hurt and disappointed I was by the loss of our friendship.

It was quite a moving piece of prose. And at the time, it felt like the only way I knew to handle the situation.

It didn't occur to me that when I started missing Annette I could have picked up the phone to invite her over to hang out with me.

I didn't think to grab her in the hallway at school to catch up on all that was going on in her life.

I didn't leave a funny note in her locker asking her to watch a movie together over the weekend.

I didn't consider any of those options because I was being *bullied* by my feelings.

I was stuck in sadness.

I was stuck in disappointment.

I was stuck in jealousy.

About the time I sent the letter, even I could recognize that the way I was behaving was pointless. It wasn't helping *me,* and it wasn't helping *us.* As I was able to see a bit more clearly, I realized that even though spending less time together did *sting* a bit, I didn't want to not have her as a friend at all.

So I gathered up my courage and approached Annette in the school cafeteria.

"Hi," I said.

I thought a saw a look of relief wash over her face.

"Hi, Chrystal," she responded hesitantly.

I'm assuming she didn't want to get green-spewed again.

"I've missed you," I said.

"Yeah," she replied, "I've been crazy busy. I had to do this huge science project with Rhonda, and then . . ."

I didn't hear any of the words after that.

Science project.

Annette and Rhonda had been spending time together because they'd been working on a project for school!

Sheesh. I suddenly felt a little foolish that I'd let my feelings get the best of me without even having all the facts. Thankfully, Annette was gracious about it and we patched up our friendship.

Y'all, when we allow it, our emotions can take us out of the game! They can really bully us. And what's so insidious

is that they're often not the best barometer of what is actually true.

I kinda learned that one the hard way.

Regardless of how we feel about what's happening in our lives, we need to learn how to interpret our emotions. Sometimes emotion comes suddenly. We realize after the fact that we have fallen into a pit and are now way underground. But many times, feelings engulf us gradually. Drifts often begin with emotions that, like strong currents, gradually carry us away. Our choice to coach ourselves through our emotions can either perpetuate the pit we find ourselves in or prevent us from sinking further.

My emotions had impacted my head. My feelings radically affected the way I saw my world. Waves of emotion overtook me, and I had sunk far enough beneath the surface that I'd been unable to breathe.

Our choice to *coach* ourselves through our emotions can either perpetuate the pit we find ourselves in or *prevent* us from sinking further.

It is your job to coach your heart. You've got to keep tabs on your emotions. When you notice your feelings trying to take you farther than it would be wise to go, you must know how to care for your heart while coaching yourself back to emotional stability.

You are not the sum of how you feel.

Some of your most difficult battles will be the tug-of-war between your head and your heart. Your heart cannot be the primary factor that determines how you live. I hate to be the one to break it to you, but your heart will lie to you and keep you from clearly seeing the truths you should act on. As Jeremiah 17:9 says, "The heart is deceitful above all things, and desperately sick; who can understand it?" (ESV).

Emotions are real, and while they should inform us, they shouldn't be in charge. If you choose to follow your heart and go with the flow of your feelings, your feelings just might pull you under. Your emotions are not equipped to lead you well.

To let your heart dictate your actions is to go dancing in a minefield.

True, we are emotional creatures.

And whether we're fourteen, sixteen, or forty-six, there are days when our hormones can be all over the place.

And by that, of course, I mean *me*.

I had some pretty extreme mood swings during my teens. And during that season, my pillow was my best friend. That navy and mauve pillowcase absorbed a lot of my heartache

To let your heart *dictate* your *actions* is to go dancing in a minefield.

over the years. When I didn't want other people to know I was having a bad day, I'd close the door to my room and sob into my pillow. I soaked that fluffy friend with my tears on the reg!

My pillow was drenched with my tears. (Not just a few drops, either. I mean *liters* of tears.)

It received my cries.

It heard the words I spoke to myself.

That faithful pillow got it all. Whatever feelings I had to bottle up to make it through the school day or youth group, were all released behind the privacy of my closed door.

What tripped me up wasn't that I had feelings. The problem was that I allowed them to boss me around. In a lot of moments, I let them keep me from the life I was designed for.

I remember going on a summer youth camp trip with my church when I was in a majorly *foul* mood. Even my circumstances—being with friends and with adults who loved me and doing fun activities—couldn't put a dent in my sour mood.

I was stuck because I'd allowed my thoughts to get the best of me. You could say that I'd *feel* my way out of a good time!

Insecurity bossed me around.

Anxiety had a chokehold on me.

The concerns I harbored crowded out joy and peace and gratitude.

Both my feelings and my thoughts kept me from enjoying what would have been a delightful experience, otherwise.

I wish I'd known then how to coach my heart, my mind, my tongue.

Part of coaching yourself through self-talk is asking yourself questions. Keep asking yourself the five W's—who, what, when, why, and where—and throw in an occasional how for good measure. When your emotions are running away and taking your head and sensibilities with them, fight for the girl in you by being willing to do the hard work of heart examination.

If I'd had these tools when I was stuck in my relationship with Annette, I could have used them to process what was going on inside of me. Coaching my heart, I might have asked:

- Why do I feel sad, lonely, and jealous?
- What has triggered these feelings in the first place?
- When did it start?
- What have I done to nurse those feelings?
- What story have I made up in my head about Annette?
- Why am I so stuck?
- What do I need to do to get unstuck?
- What facts do I actually have?

Sometimes those questions might be too much for you to process on your own.

It's okay if you need help from a friend or a licensed counselor to work through issues and identify appropriate responses based on healthy thoughts and beliefs. And it's

okay if you can't get to the root of your emotions in one conversation. Swimming against the current is hard work.

Nothing is wrong with understanding your heart, experiencing the emotions of the heart, and caring for your heart.
You just can't live acting on the demands of the heart. If you
allow your heart to lead your actions, you just might act in
ways that hurt yourself or others.

I'm delighted to report that I've learned a lot about myself
and my emotions since then.

A few months ago I had an exchange with someone I
love that felt like a punch in the gut. I felt as if a dagger had
been thrust through my heart.

I felt sad.

I felt angry.

I coddled and nurtured those feelings.

I let my heart rule my head.

I let my feelings bully the rest of me.

When my eyes were opened to the ways I was behaving
in response to the hurt I'd experienced, I decided to do something about it.

I expressed some of what I was experiencing in my journal.

I processed other thoughts verbally with someone I trusted.

I invited my husband and a close friend to help me uncover
the reasons for my reactions.

But I didn't stop there. I rehearsed the truth of the love
I believed in my head. I recalled God's love for me and His
forgiveness. I remembered how unlovable and how hurtful
I'd been to others in my life, people who continued to love

me despite the pain I caused them. Slowly but surely, I talked myself down off the ledge and worked through my emotional response. Remembering God's love for me helped me to decide—apart from my emotions—how best to show love and forgiveness toward the person who had hurt me.

I learned how to feel without letting my emotions rule.

Feel fully, but don't let your heart lead you to hurt yourself or others. Process your emotions. Work through the hard stuff by yourself or with someone you trust. But never forget: although emotions can guide you, they shouldn't govern you.

It took me longer than I would have liked to discover that the way I feel isn't always the barometer of what is true.

When I was a little girl, I thought that all adults had life *figured out.*

I now know that's not true.

Most of the women I know today are grownup girls who've learned a tad about how to adult. And we wake up every day and do the best we can do. The ones who are thriving are the ones who notice their feelings, honor them, and coach their hearts.

> The way you *feel* isn't always the barometer of what is *true.*

To receive truth.
To speak truth.
To choose truth.
To dwell in truth.

They've learned how to coach their hearts, and you can too.

Reflections for the Rescue

REMEMBER

You are not the sum of how you feel.

REFLECT

- Has your heart ever led you astray? Did you know the truth, or did you ignore it?
- Are you an emotional "sharer" or an emotional "stuffer"? What could be helpful and hurtful about each?
- How best do you process your emotions? Alone or with a friend? Talking it out or writing it down? Slow and easy or fast and furious?

RESPOND

The next time you are experiencing a strong emotion, hold it in the light of truth. Ask yourself the five W's—who, what, when, why, and where—and evaluate how you feel in light of God's Word. Then act on truth.

PSALM 26:2; JEREMIAH 17:9; JOHN 8:32;
EPHESIANS 6:14; 1 JOHN 1:5–9

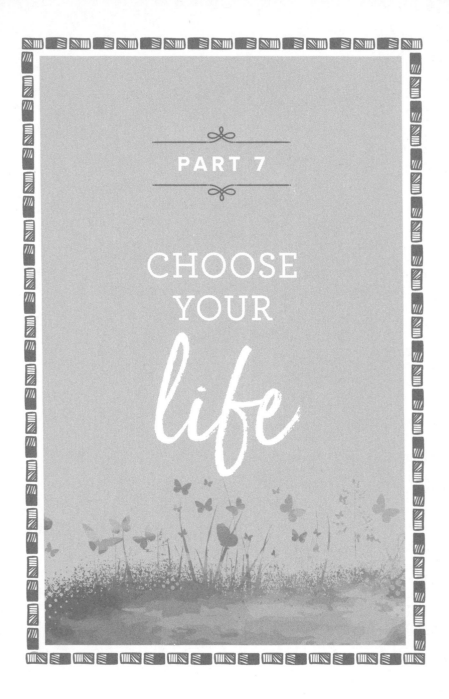

PART 7

CHOOSE
YOUR
life

CHAPTER 28

When It's Time to Party

Choose celebration

Y ou already know that I proudly sported a Target-red T-shirt when I worked as a retail associate during high school.

Though I doubt they provide it anymore, back in the day employees at the Tar-JAY got a forty percent discount off anything we bought in the store. (Even if you're not a math person, you can calculate that forty percent is a deep discount! If not, just take my word for it.)

Whenever I'd be hanging up clothes that people left in the dressing room, stocking the jewelry spinners, or organizing the home décor section, I'd often see something special that I'd like to purchase. In most cases, I had the money. I could have bought the skirt and the earrings and the bulletin board whenever I pleased.

But I didn't.

I didn't buy whatever struck my fancy because I had

goals. I was saving my money for college, and I was proud that my savings account was growing.

So instead of gratifying myself by spending my whole paycheck on awesome stuff, I chose to practice restraint. Specifically, I would set small goals to reward myself for making progress on the big goal of saving money for college.

After I earn $40, I'll buy the lip stain for $4.

Once I save $200, I'll buy this shirt for $20.

I'd enjoy these little wins along the way to reaching my larger goals.

That's what I want to encourage you to do.

I've asked you to commit to believing the truth about who God says you are.

I've asked you to pay close attention to the road ahead of you.

I've asked you to do the work of discovering the unique, amazing, one-of-a-kind girl you are.

I've asked you to care for your heart, your mind, your soul, your body.

I've asked you to keep your eyes on the prize.

I've asked you to exercise discipline.

Basically, I've asked you to work hard to honor the girl inside as you become the woman God created you to be.

That takes energy.

It takes focus.

It takes commitment.

And that's why I also believe you should pause along the way and celebrate what is right in your life.

Practice gratitude.

Notice those places where you're succeeding.

Stop to celebrate little victories.

You deserve it.

And when you stop to name the ways you are flourishing, it is like putting gas in your tank for the drive ahead.

By the time spring rolls around, you might be so ready for summer vacation that you don't pause to appreciate the fact that *you made it through another school year!* You did it. It's an accomplishment. So, celebrate.

> Eat pancakes at McDonald's.
>
> Wear a gold medal to school.
>
> Put a big crazy sign in front of your house congratulating yourself for being promoted to tenth grade.
>
> Drink *two* Dr. Peppers. (Yeah, I know, it just got crazy up in here.)

I also want you to celebrate the wins that can too easily be disguised as losses.

You didn't make first chair violin, but you advanced to second chair.

Celebrate.

You weren't elected as president of the student body, but as runner up you will serve as vice president.

Celebrate.

A lot of other people haven't accomplished what you have accomplished. So pause to name and honor what you've achieved.

The win for you might not be the kind of accomplishment that will ever show up on a college application. But it's still a win.

If you're a girl who likes to read, keep a running list of the books you've completed and then cook a word-themed dinner for your family before a big night of Scrabble. (Think alphabet soup, cookies shaped like letters, etc.)

I also want you to name the victories that might not look like a win to anyone else; honor those.

Do you struggle to not talk back to your parents or hassle your siblings?

Celebrate a "No Negativity" day by bringing home a box of ice cream sandwiches for your family to enjoy.

The comedian Jerry Seinfeld would mark an "X" on his calendar every day he created a new joke. When a younger comic asked him about his secrets to success, Seinfeld suggested he get a calendar, write a joke each day, and enjoy the satisfaction of marking that "X." He coached him by saying that after awhile he wouldn't want to break the chain.[9]

What's a tangible way for you to see your progress?

If you're training for a half-marathon, maybe you put a chart on the fridge to mark your progress.

If you're determined to make better choices about food—either healthier individual choices if you love the junk food, or more plentiful choices if you're tempted to restrict—consider treating yourself to the purchase of cute shoes when you reach your goal.

If you struggle to get to school on time, because you stay up too late at night binge studying, put an "X" on that calendar for every night you turn off your lights and phone

by 10:30. (I know it's harder to turn off your brain, but it's a good start!) Reward yourself after 10 "X"s.

The big win is choosing to see where you're winning, where you're succeeding, where you're growing, and giving thanks for it.

Last day of summer school classes? Go to a water park.

Your soccer team made it to regionals? Invite the girls on your team over for a pizza party.

Memorize an entire book of the Bible? Eat ice cream. (Don't ask me why that's the reward. It just is.)

Choosing celebration is a great way to practice gratitude, thanking God for the blessings, gifts, growth, and achievements along the way. You don't have to win Olympic gold to recognize all the little wins on your journey.

You know that you can be successful, right?

You can.

It's going to look different for you than it does for me.

It's going to look different for me than it does for my daughter Kariss.

And it's going to look different for Kariss than it does for you.

But you have everything you need to succeed at that thing the Lord has created you for. Noticing the wins along the way is proof of it!

When you celebrate, you look back with gratitude at where you've been and what you've done—and you look forward with expectation to all the possibilities in your future. Celebration is a tool that helps you continue to hope.

Celebration is the way you mark the moments of your life. It involves heartfelt experiences that create lasting memories. Those memories are the building blocks for your perception of your existence on this earth.

You might be good at acknowledging a remarkable person or event in a culminating moment, but *you* are also a remarkable person, and your life is an ongoing remarkable event worthy of being celebrated along the way.

You are a *remarkable* person, and your life is an ongoing remarkable event worthy of being *celebrated* along the way.

When we dismiss our progress, we miss the opportunity to remind ourselves we are capable and adept at achieving a favorable outcome. And we unintentionally shame our girl into taking two steps backward.

Once you begin to celebrate your small achievements, you begin to accept that you are capable of doing it again. So set small goals. Aspire. Dream. Live with intention, even if you limit your ideas or plans to the next ninety days. That will give you something to aim for and a moment you can mark with thankfulness, acknowledgment, and maybe a tiny bit of personal partying—you know, with sparkling grape juice or something.

I recently listened to a podcast where Lisa Nichols, a motivational speaker, said: "Don't get attached to the number of times you fall down. Get attached to the number of times you get back up again."

The moment I heard her words, I knew I'd slowly become attached to falling down. Instead of celebrating the times I've restarted, tried again, or inched forward, I'd developed the habit of looking for defeat because it somehow seemed easier to find. But it was only easier to find because I'd been practicing looking for it.

When you choose to celebrate and be thankful, no matter how bad you think things are, you set the stage for more of the same.

So let's mark our moments. Find something—anything—to express gratitude for. Take notice of the milestones, achievements, and the good in the everyday. In so doing, we will encourage more of the same.

When I was turning seventeen, I wanted to have a cool birthday party.

I don't mean balloons and pin-the-tail-on-the-donkey and rainbow sprinkles on my Wonder Woman cake. I mean I wanted to have the kind of party kids wanted to be at—with music and dancing and no parents.

I was psyched when my dad said I could have a party, but we had very different visions for how it would go down.

He was still imagining pinning a tail on a farm animal.

No matter how bad you think things are, give thanks.

Though I did nix the donkey game, I decided that having a party was better than no party.

Because my birthday is in July, we set up picnic tables in the backyard with red, white, and blue tablecloths. My mom made baked beans, potato salad, hamburgers with all the fixins, homemade ice cream, and 7-Up cake. And, because I had no way to stop him, my dad was in charge of games.

So I need you to imagine all of my friends playing tag, in the heat of a Texas July, running circles around the outside of our house. It wasn't just regular tag, it was more like a relay race my dad had made up.

As I watched it unfold, I could only think, *This is so boring. It's totally whack. Why can't I just be like everyone else?*

But then I heard one of my best friends laughing. And I noticed that my sixteen-, seventeen-, and eighteen-year-old friends looked like they were having a ball.

So I chilled.

I decided to celebrate anyway.

And, I kid you not, to this day my friends still say it was the most fun party they ever attended.

Perhaps more important, it's one of the days that *I* remember most from my adolescence.

How you celebrate isn't as important as the fact that you *do* celebrate.

So just do it.

If you think it sounds corny—and I get that it might—I want you to trust me and believe that celebrating is an important marker in your journey toward becoming *you*.

Reflections for the Rescue

REMEMBER

Celebration is the way you mark the moments of your life.

REFLECT

- Does celebration come naturally to you? Why or why not?
- When do you take time to celebrate? Do you only celebrate major milestones like birthdays, anniversaries, and special occasions, or do you celebrate something every day?
- What could celebrating every day look like?

RESPOND

Spend time today noting what's right in your life. As a part of your reflection, thank God for what's right in your life. Practice gratitude.

PSALM 95:2; COLOSSIANS 4:2; COLOSSIANS 3:17; LUKE 15:11–24; EXODUS 12:14; NEHEMIAH 8:9–10; 1 CHRONICLES 29:20–22; PSALM 100

CHAPTER 29

Opting for Light and Air

Choose honesty

My favorite dress in sixth grade was grey with maroon print. Tea length, trimmed with a maroon edge, it had a thin grey fabric belt that I tied neatly in a bow. I *loved* it, and I wore it all the time, with black hose.

I was a vision, and really thought I was something else in that dress.

After English class, I was walking down the stairs to the first level of the school when I lost my footing. I tumbled down about five stairs and landed at the bottom of the stairwell.

No broken bones, but my pride was pretty bruised. And I ripped those pantyhose right above the hem of my dress.

Thankfully, only one girl saw the awkward debacle unfold.

"Are you okay?" she asked, as she moved toward me.

I tried to play it off like I loved falling down stairs.

"Yeah!" I said with a chipper tone. "I'm good. It's all good. Thanks!"

I kind of made it sound like I'd planned it.

I breathed a little prayer that she wouldn't tell anyone else what she'd witnessed.

About halfway through my next class, the adrenaline that had helped me hop up off the floor with a smile on my face began to wane. My knee began to throb. And the rip in my hose seemed to be growing by the minute, even though I completely ignored it. Before science was over, it had exploded into a huge gaping hole, exposing my light brown skin.

After the bell rang to dismiss class, a kid who sat behind me asked, "Do you realize you have a hole . . . ?"

"Yeah," I said with a little lilt in my voice. "I know. Thanks!"

Because I was also now limping, my teacher called me to her desk.

"Chrystal, are you okay?" she asked.

When I explained how I'd hurt my knee she sent me to the nurse's office, who made me lie down and put ice on it.

I'd tried to cover up.

Have you?

Have you had an imperfection or a rip or a pain that you tried desperately to hide from others?

Did you try to mask it until it got too obvious to hide?

I get it.

Believe me, I do.

I wanted to control other people's perceptions of me. I wanted to pretend like I had my stuff together. Pretend that I wasn't imperfect. Pretend that I wasn't hurting. Pretend that I wasn't broken.

Ultimately, I failed.

And when I could no longer pretend, that's when my healing began.

Other times, though, we can be pretty successful at projecting an image of ourselves that we want others to see. Of course, I mean selfies.

Most of us have taken them. Some of us have taken them seriously.

If you've ever posted a selfie on social media, you can appreciate the work it takes to get a good one. The lighting has to be right. The angle has to be right. And Lord knows the filter has to be right.

Selfies are serious business.

I'm embarrassed to say there have been times I took thirty snaps to get the one photo I felt represented what I wanted others to see.

Most of us have snapshots of our lives we don't care for others to see. We prefer to present that one picture taken in the right light, at the right angle, and with the right filter. Yet when we care too much, it makes us unwilling to be vulnerable and authentic. So, instead, we edit out the parts of ourselves we don't want others to see.

We enter into the great cover-up.

We cover up by wearing a smile and convincing everyone we're okay, even though we feel like we're shrinking on the inside.

We cover up that we feel lonely and are longing to be known, and we continue to live in isolation.

We cover up by being good at religion even though we really aren't good with God, and we remain distant, detached, and disinterested.

Just like that girl in the garden of Eden, our first instinct is to cover up our mistakes, to hide our faults, frustrations, and shame. Our greatest cover-ups happen when we convince ourselves that if no one can see our struggle, then it's not real.

The cover-up can kill your commitment. It can suffocate you and cease your participation in the very process that will save your life.

You also may be tempted to disguise defeat by wearing a mask.

> The cover-up can kill your *commitment.* It can suffocate you and cease your *participation* in the very process that will *save your life.*

Sometimes the realities we're hiding are more serious than the rogue zit or ripped tights.

One girl pulls her sleeves down over the marks on her arms where she's been cutting.

Another girl does the same to hide track marks.

One girl turns up the volume on the television because she doesn't want others to hear what she's doing in the bathroom.

One girl, who's begun to believe that the world would

be better off without her, tells no one that she's plagued by these oppressive thoughts.

Another keeps Altoids in her purse, trying to cover the smell of alcohol on her breath.

Still another wears a constant smile to mask the physical or sexual hurt that was inflicted by someone she trusted.

If you don't feel like opening up to your parents or friends is a safe choice, find someone with whom you can get real.

It might be a counselor at school.

It could be a youth minister or youth group volunteer.

It might even be the parent of a friend.

Find someone you trust to help you work through the hurt you've tried to hide.

I know that probably sounds like the very last thing you want to do. I hear that. But when we cover up our wounds, they can get infected. Physical wounds heal when they're exposed to light and air. The same is true of our emotional hurts. They need light and air to heal.

Each of us is bound to fall. And when we do, when we get scraped and bruised and bloodied, how will we respond?

Will we seek the care of healers, committing ourselves to health?

Or will we attempt to hide the brokenness?

Precious one, don't settle for the great cover-up.

Take off the mask, the one you've been hiding behind for a long time. Be prepared that when you do, it can hurt. The light burns, and the fresh air feels uncomfortable. Acknowledging your tears leaves you open to criticism and judgment by those who have no idea what it means to walk in your shoes.

But in the process, you will open yourself up to freedom.

When you reject the great cover-up, you also reject a weight that's kept you burdened by a lie. When you take off the mask, acknowledge your tears, and reject the cover-up, you will be able to breathe.

You will live in the light. You will live free.

Reflections for the Rescue

REMEMBER

Don't get comfortable in the cover-up.

REFLECT

- Take a moment to think about what you may be hiding. What do you not want people to know? Why are you afraid to be known?
- How is the cover-up working for you? What has happened in your head and in your heart as you hide guilt, shame, embarrassment, or self-consciousness?
- What do you think it will look like for you to live in the light? Who will help you take off the mask? When?

RESPOND

Name a person, and name a date. Be brave and hold yourself to your unmasking.

❦

1 JOHN 1:6–10; ISAIAH 43:18–19; ROMANS 8:1; HEBREWS 8:12; PSALM 32:5; JAMES 5:16; PROVERBS 28:13; ROMANS 3:23; MATTHEW 7:5; COLOSSIANS 1:21–22; ACTS 19:18

CHAPTER 30

Having Her Back

Choose community

There's an intriguing documentary on Netflix about world champion tennis players Venus and Serena Williams. I've watched it four times so far.

It's so interesting to me how two girls from the same family can both be world champions. I'm fascinated by the dynamics of their upbringing, their training, and their paths to success. But more than anything, I'm fascinated by the dynamics of their relationship.

These girls are sisters. They both desire to be at the top of their game, but that also means they regularly compete against each other. But while each girl shows up with a strong desire to come home with the first-place trophy, her fight for first does not trump this most important truth: they are sisters. Those two girls love each other deeply, and each wants to see the other succeed.

In one scene of the documentary, a reporter asks Venus how she feels after Serena beats her in a match. Venus replies, "Of course I want to win, but at the end of the day, both of us share the same last name. Serena is my sister. If one of us wins, we both win."[10]

These sisters don't let competition define their relationship. They challenge and coach each other. They serve (pun intended) and support one another. They give each other the freedom to pursue individual goals while making sure that they face the world together.

They are sisters.

They know they have their own games to play, but they don't forget the importance of accountability, motivation, and love in their relationship.

That's what sisters do.

They share.

They hold each other's hand.

They encourage.

Sisterhood is what Venus and Serena were made for.

It's what I was made for.

And it's what you were made for.

Too often, something outside of us, and something *inside* of us, tells us that other girls and women are our "competition."

We envy the number of likes her selfie from the football game got.

We notice when guys notice her.

We compare our silhouette to hers.

We feel a little good inside when our class rank is higher than hers.

Ick, right?!

It's not who I want to be and I'm assuming it's not who

you want to be. Yet we're tempted daily to try to be a little better than the next girl.

We were made for so much more.

God designed us to love one another, and when we do, we thrive and those around us thrive.

So instead of looking at other girls as if they're your competition, I want you to throw away that distorted filter—which is sort of like looking at the world through muddy sunglasses—and choose to see others the way God sees them.

As women, we are playing for the same team. And as teammates, as sisters, we are all better off when we support one another.

Recently, we've seen the power of sisterhood through the #metoo movement. A campaign against sexual harassment and assault, the hashtag has raised awareness by communicating the magnitude of the problems women face. Honesty and vulnerability have made us stronger together than staying silent.

We're stronger when we band together.

And standing together in unity, determining to be honest with one another, isn't something that begins when you're in a college sorority.

It starts now.

Supporting your friends is something that you can be doing right now. (Of all the assignments I'm giving in this book, this one may be the most fun. Just sayin'.)

Does your friend play on the school softball team? I'm going to go out on a limb and guess that the softball bleachers are not spilling over with fans. Show up at the next home softball game to cheer for your friend. Maybe make a goofy sign to hang on the fence. Be your friend's cheerleader.

Now I'm gonna push you even further than softball and soccer, basketball and lacrosse. Do you have a friend who's a mathlete? (Yeah, I went there.) Or one who's a member of the school debate team? Or science Olympiad? Dress up in school colors, show up with your pompoms, and give them a clap!

Does your church have a youth group? Grab a few of those friends who attend your school and choose a morning to meet before school to pray for each other. Give every girl five minutes to review her previous week and preview the coming one, so you know how to pray. Pray for each other and then follow up on the requests when you see your friends in the hallways. Be your friends' *spiritual* cheerleader.

One of the best places for you to find—or build!—the kind of community that nurtures your soul and others' is through church.

My husband and I have two daughters who were not down with youth group in middle school. For whatever reason, it just wasn't their thing. I considered *making* them go and I do support families who make that choice, but it wasn't the right move for our family.

When the girls got to tenth grade, they gave youth group another try. This time, they dug it. On Wednesday nights they'd go for dinner and then activities.

Jessica made new friends.

Kariss tried new activities.

Both girls grew their faith by going a little deeper and participating in a book study.

Hear me: I'm not encouraging you to be more active in your church because I want you to be busy. I'm sure you already have lots of activities to keep you busy.

I want you to find a community where you can love and support other girls and young women and where you can find that support for yourself. We were designed for community, and it is a good gift from God.

This is one of those places where I want to give you a sneak peek into the trajectory—in this case, a social trajectory—that many women experience.

I think it's fair to say that when we're younger, having the time and space and energy to nurture friendships isn't difficult.

We play together at daycare or preschool or the playground or the YMCA.

When we get to elementary school, we giggle and play at lunchtime, recess, and at our afterschool activities.

In middle school we get to ride the bus to basketball games, track meets, and fieldtrips.

In high school we spend time with friends at church, Friday night football games, the mall, and McDonald's.

In college we get to hang out with our friends in the dorms and student center and maybe even a sorority. We get spoiled when we only have to walk a few feet down the hall to borrow a sweater or boots or jewelry.

When we're younger, we often enjoy the benefits of community because it's built into the rhythm of our daily lives.

A lot of women I know have found that developing a strong sisterhood of women becomes a little more difficult starting in our mid-twenties.

One woman went to grad school that didn't have on-campus housing, making it harder to connect outside of school.

One got married and moved across the country for her husband's job.

One woman bought a house in the suburbs where she didn't even know her neighbors' names.

Another lived in an urban high-rise where she'd only see her neighbors a few moments each day on the elevator.

So a lot of women in their twenties and thirties find that it does take more effort to connect with their women friends in that season.

But you know what?

I don't know one woman who wouldn't say that making the effort to be together and love each other—whether it's grabbing coffee, cheering a friend on as she finishes a marathon, or bringing her a celebration cupcake when she gets a promotion—isn't worth it.

It is worth the effort.

We were not meant to journey through this life alone. Find someone in your world who can encourage you (real life is best, but virtual will do). Find someone whom you can encourage. Hold her hand. Share your stories.

Women I know who failed to value and nurture friendships when they were younger will testify to the value of cultivating sisterhood *now*. Some of the relationships in which you're investing now may even become lifelong sister circles.

Showing up and supporting your sisters works a lot like

> We were not meant to *journey* through this life *alone*.

making friends does. Nothing is gained by waiting at home and whining that no one cares for you.

You need to go get it.

Show up for your community.

Nourish the girl who's hungry for a friend.

Bless the girl who needs a win.

When another girl succeeds, give her a clap.

Pour into your community and see how it pours into you.

I want to challenge you to create a sister circle—a group of friends who are committed to being your cheerleaders. You don't have to have a large circle of sisters to know the beauty of support, compassion, or even tough love. And don't assume that the friendships you have now will end after you toss your graduation caps in the air. A friend who's almost a decade ahead of me was in high school in the mid-1990s. (I know, I know, that's like a million years ago.) Well, inspired by the Prince lyrics, "Tonight we're gonna party like it's 1999," her sister circle made a commitment when they were seventeen, that they were going to get together on December 31, 1999. Many of them would be thirty years old! (Which, of course, is like being a *million* years old.) On New Year's Eve of the new millennia, their circle gathered—single women and married ones, ones with babies and those without, from all over the country. Today theirs is a circle that has supported one another through promotions and job losses, marriages and divorces, deaths of parents and friends, and even the births and deaths of children.

That's what sisters do for each other.

So commit to at least one or two girls or young women in your life. Strive for long-haul relationships, the kind that are deep and real. Take the development of the sisters in your circle seriously. Celebrate your sister. Support her as she runs her race. Be a safe place for her to take off her mask.

Move forward in life while keeping an eye on your sister to make sure she's moving too.

We are ultimately alive not for ourselves, but for one another.

And know this: when she wins, you both win.

Reflections for the Rescue

REMEMBER

Believe in the concept of community.

REFLECT

- As you read this chapter, what feelings or thoughts came to mind about your own sister circle?
- If you don't have a sister circle, think about who or where your sister circle might be. Be open if God puts someone on your mind.
- How can you be more intentional about encouraging your sister friends to honor their lives? How can your friends help you to honor your own?

RESPOND

Take time right now to text one or two of your girls to set a time to meet up. Friendship matters.

———————— ❧ ————————

HEBREWS 10:24–25; PSALM 133:1; 1 PETER 3:8; MATTHEW 18:20; COLOSSIANS 3:14; 1 JOHN 4:11; 1 JOHN 3:16–17

CHAPTER 31

The Butterfly Effect

Dare to believe change is possible

S cience is not my thing. I have issues with the experiments. They don't work or I'm missing some needed item or the experiment is a little messy or straight-up gross.

I don't mind experiments in general. I just don't want to be in charge of them.

But there's one experiment I've done three times now that I kind of enjoy.

The butterfly garden.

This experiment, watching caterpillars turn into butterflies, is more like an experience.

I most recently did this experiment with my youngest son. When I gathered all the books and supplies he needed for the school year, he saw the box for the butterfly garden and was excited to know that this year he'd have his turn. He spent all year talking about it, and when the time came in early spring, we sent for our caterpillars via mail order.

When the caterpillars arrived, they came in a closed container. No mess for me. Hallelujah.

For a few days, we watched those caterpillars move around the covered plastic cup ever so slowly. Eating, crawling, and eating some more. For a little over a week, the caterpillars stayed in constant, steady-yet-slow motion, but to my little kindergartener son, nothing was happening.

He was looking for a butterfly.

At his age, he understood the concept of time, but each day seemed like an eternity to him, especially when he was looking forward to seeing the butterfly emerge from its chrysalis and fly around our little netted garden in all its glory.

The process of the caterpillar turning into a butterfly was simply taking too long. So long that he started to wonder if the transformation would ever happen.

"Mom, are you *sure* that these caterpillars are going to turn into butterflies?"

"Yes, baby. I'm sure."

Next day. Same question. Different format.

"Mom, why aren't the caterpillars turning into butterflies? *How long* is this gonna take?"

"Son, they will turn into butterflies. It'll just take a little while longer."

A few days later, the caterpillars made their way to the top of the plastic container and hung from the lid. Within twenty-four hours, the chrysalises had formed and the caterpillars were perfectly still and seemingly lifeless.

"Mom, are the caterpillars dead?"

"No, son, they aren't dead. They're turning into butterflies."

"But Mom, *nothing's happening!*"

I could totally see why my son would think that.

After days of slow movement, the caterpillars had hidden away, become totally still, and nothing appeared to be happening at all.

But I had a vantage point that my son didn't have.

I had done this experiment before with my two older sons; I knew what to expect. I knew that the transformation he wanted to see would take some time, and that patience would be required.

I knew if my kindergartner could just hold on a little while longer, he would see butterflies emerge. He just needed to hang in there and believe.

It took a while, but we watched, faithfully expecting something beautiful to be born.

When nothing was happening, we watched.

When the change was taking forever, we watched.

When there was no movement, we watched.

We watched, waited, and eventually witnessed the miracle of metamorphosis.

The butterfly slowly but surely made its way out of the chrysalis, struggling to break free from all that had constrained it but was necessary to create its beauty. And from that struggle, the butterfly gained the strength it needed to fly.

I know that as I've shared my heart with you in this book, you might easily believe me because you've been through your own process and seen what happens when you hang in there and hold onto hope for the life of the girl in you. I hope you've been encouraged, inspired, and motivated to live with a clear vision of the beautiful soul God has given you.

But I also know that you might be like my son, wanting

to see what comes next, but frustrated that those changes in your life are happening so slowly—or don't appear to be happening at all.

You might be wondering if God sees you—if He knows that you feel buried deep down below the surface of what should be your life and if He actually intends to help you make your way there.

You might very well want to see yourself operating in the fullness and beauty of the girl God created you to be, but because you struggle or because change is happening slowly or because no one watching your life appears to believe in your life, you may not be sure a life that matters is within your reach.

You may be like my son and find yourself hesitant to believe because you've never seen it. You may not ever have seen the process completed in the life of someone you know.

But I have.

So I'd like to ask you to trust me.

I'd like to ask you to believe that since I've seen it in my own life and in the lives of others, a beautiful future is possible for you.

Embrace the process of your progress.

Focus on pouring yourself fully into the decisions you need to make, and then doing whatever it takes to stick with your chosen direction.

Use discernment in the people, places, and things in your life.

Exercise the discipline necessary to dig deep to become the girl you were always meant to be.

I'm praying as I write this chapter that when the process of your progress gets too hard, feels too long, or seems to cost too much, you'll do what it takes to coach yourself back to the truths you believe. And I pray that you'll celebrate along the way, showing gratitude for small accomplishments, little victories, and every baby step you take. I'm also hoping you'll put more effort into focusing on your own two feet rather than comparing yourself with the people around you.

And if you fall, I'm cheering for you to get back up, own your story, and continue your journey, resisting the cover-up that often accompanies shame and guilt.

I invite you to show up for your life—being, believing, and becoming the person God knew you could be when He planted His gifts in you.

Embrace and expect that your process will not be perfect, but trust that God can use even your drifts, decisions, and collisions as soil in which something beautiful can grow and bloom.

Most important, I hope you see now that even beautiful lives—*especially* beautiful lives—require work.

There's no shortcut to doing the work of nourishing your soul, taking care of your body, and participating with the work of God's Spirit in you. While you need to know truth and understand truth, you have to do the work of operating

God can use even your drifts, decisions, and collisions as *soil* in which something beautiful can *grow* and *bloom*.

in truth, however long it takes or however difficult that process might be. Every bit of your process and all the work you put in will be worth it when you see the beauty that emerges in you as you partner with God's design and plan for your life.

❧

Beautiful girl, every struggle you have will help you develop the strength you need to fly. You are capable. You have the right to hope and dream. And I want excitement to bubble up in you as you realize that you, my friend, get a turn.

I am asking you to believe in the butterfly effect at work in you.

> Wait for it.
> Watch for it.
> Work for it.
> Hope for it.
> Pray for it.
> Dare to believe. Change is possible.

And this is what I know for sure about the girl you want to be or the girl you didn't know you could be: she's inside you and she's ready to fly.

❧

*"Well, I can't describe her exactly—
except to say that she was beautiful.
She was—tremendously alive."*

—F. Scott Fitzgerald

Reflections for the Rescue

REMEMBER

Every struggle you have will help you
develop the strength you need.

REFLECT

- What is your next step after reading this book?
  What are you motivated to do?
- What thoughts or actions do you need to change
  today to honor the life of the girl in you?
- What is your dream for the girl in you? What are
  you daring to believe?

RESPOND

Seal the deal. Take time to marinate on the message
of this book *for you*. Journal about your dreams,
make a list of your goals, or pray about the next
steps. Be motivated enough to take action. Then
share your plan of action with a sister friend.

PSALM 51:10; EZEKIEL 36:26; 2 CORINTHIANS
3:17–18; 2 CORINTHIANS 5:17; EPHESIANS 4:23–24;
TITUS 3:5; ROMANS 8:29; ROMANS 12:2

Acknowledgments

So grateful to Carolyn McCready and Annette Bourland for believing in this message for young women. You both ensured that my heart for girls of all ages reached further than even I could see.

Thankful and in awe of Margot Starbuck—her gift with words and her gift in encouraging people. Your writing is impeccable and your ability to move my thoughts and language to the heart of the matter is both uncanny and clever, wrapped with the bow of warmth and friendship.

Grateful for my parents, Drs. Tony and Lois Evans, who cheered me on as a girl and who still cheer me on as a grown woman. You've never stopped encouraging me to show up for my life.

And to my husband, Jessie, who has always championed me honoring the life of the girl in me—thank you for the freedom to do so.

Notes

Chapter 5

1. Gretchen Rubin, "Quiz: Are You Drifting?" *GretchenRubin
.com*, July 22, 2009, http://gretchenrubin.com/happiness_
project/2009/07/quiz-are-you-drifting/. Accessed November
2016.

Chapter 6

2. Nicholas Bakalar, "37.2 Trillion: Galaxies or Human Cells?"
New York Times, June 19, 2015, https://www.nytimes.com/
2015/06/23/science/37-2-trillion-galaxies-or-human-cells
.html. Accessed January 2017.

Chapter 9

3. Steven Furtick, *@stevenfurtick*, May 10, 2011, https://twitter
.com/stevenfurtick/status/67981913746444288. Accessed
November 2016.

Chapter 10

4. Elisabeth Elliot, *Discipline: The Glad Surrender,* (Revell:
Grand Rapids, MI, 2006): 43–44.

Chapter 16

5. Naomi Blumberg, "Misty Copeland: American Dancer,"
Encyclopaedia Britannica, October 5, 2016, https://www

.britannica.com/biography/Misty-Copeland. Accessed
January 2017.

Chapter 20

6. "Lee Iacocca Quotes," *BrainyQuote.com*, (n.d.), http://www
.brainyquote.com/quotes/quotes/l/leeiacocca149249.html.
Accessed November 2016.

Chapter 23

7. Denzel Washington, director, *The Great Debaters* (motion
picture), 2007.

Chapter 26

8. "Dr. Maya Angelou—Power of Words," *Oprah Presents
Master Class*, https://youtu.be/8PXdacSqvcA.

Chapter 28

9. Gina Trapani, "Jerry Seinfeld's Productivity Secret,"
Lifehacker.com, July 24, 2007, https://lifehacker.com/
281626/jerry-seinfelds-productivity-secret.

Chapter 30

10. Maiken Baird and Michelle Major, directors, *Venus and
Serena* (motion picture), Magnolia Pictures, 2012.